Illingworth

STEVENSON, Mike

Illingworth : a biography

B/ILL

**Please return this book
on or before the last
date shown or ask for
it to be renewed.**

7/12

♻ 100% recycled paper.

L32

- 9 DEC 2002

Blackpool

11/1/13

D1348101

Illingworth

A Biography by Mike Stevenson

BAR/ADL

WARD LOCK LIMITED   LONDON

796. 358 '092 /ILL

Front cover illustration by Patrick Eagar

Produced by Midas Books for Ward Lock Ltd

© Mike Stevenson 1978

ISBN 0 7063 5677 2 Paperback Edition

This edition first published in Great Britain in 1978 by Ward Lock Limited,
116 Baker Street, London W1M 2BB, a member of the Pentos Group.

Filmset in Plantin by The Humble Wordsmith, Tonbridge, Kent.
Printed in Great Britain by offset lithography by
Billing & Sons Ltd, Guildford, London and Worcester

To my wife, friend and secretary, Biddy and all those who have helped so generously with this book, especially Raymond Illingworth.

Contents

List of Illustrations

Foreword

The only questions about a biography of Raymond Illingworth
were who would write it, and when. Certainly it needed to be
written, for he has been one of the most important figures in a
period of profound change in cricket. He has never sought
publicity, never appealed to the more meretricious star-makers;
indeed, he might be described as the most under-estimated
captain of our time. That is not to say that he has not been
accorded both admiration and respect, but it is arguable that he
still has not had as much credit as he has deserved. Anyone — or
almost anyone — can captain a team of outstanding performers;
but Raymond Illingworth's achievement with the England side
of his time was quite outstanding. It was once described as
'papering over the cracks' but it was much more than that. Paper
does not hold brick walls together, and his team often revealed
astounding resilience and resistance against opposition which,
taken man for man, was obviously more powerful.

Something similar might be said about the successes of
Leicestershire who, under his captaincy, often reached levels
higher than the apparent sum of their abilities. In both cases it is
possible to attribute results to Illingworth's outstanding tactical
acumen. That, though, is not the full explanation. It is also true
that, like Sir Alf Ramsey in another field, he has the knack of
choosing men he can motivate so that, within his team, they are
more effective than elsewhere.

At the point when he left Yorkshire it seemed that his career at
the top level was ended. Surely, even he did not foresee the most
rewarding period of his cricketing life still ahead of him. So,
though, it has proved.

To understand so complicated and thoroughly Yorkshire a
person as Raymond Illingworth — it has always seemed to me
significant that his Yorkshire contemporaries called him
Raymond and not Ray — his biographer needed a northern

understanding. All but the few miles between Chinley and High Neb, Mike Stevenson was born in Yorkshire. At least he was close enough to look in; for some time he actually taught the young of Yorkshire — among other things — cricket. Much of his own cricket has been played in that county or about its boundaries, and for many years now he has reported and broadcast northern matches. Thus he has ample knowledge of atmosphere and setting. More importantly, he had the will to understand and genuine enthusiasm to write about his most rewarding subject.

JOHN ARLOTT

Foreword

To understand Ray Illingworth you must first discover the deep-set heart of Yorkshire professionalism, a rewarding exercise for Mike Stevenson the biographer.

The pen may not dash away into purple descriptions of devil-may-care cricket. Rather, it must pursue that certain doggedness of character and the quiet devotion to cricket's skills. It must tell of Yorkshire and England matches lost and won, but it must also portray the Yorkshireman's innate faith in a game which sends his Dad off to oil his bat on a dark January morning before going to work and his Mam off to the matches with scorebook under her arm.

How do you paint a mountain which stands dark and solid? You probe the fascinating nooks, watch the hues alter in differing conditions and wait patiently for the sunny moments to reveal its surprising beauty. Mike Stevenson's study of the outwardly phlegmatic Ray Illingworth does just that.

Understanding Ray Illingworth is to understand Arthur Mitchell, Emmott Robinson, Doug Padgett or David Bairstow. Some in the long line have been more talkative than others, but in words or silence the true Yorkshire professional knows about cricket and assumes that you know better now that he has told you . . . 'tha' knows'.

Did the transfer to Leicestershire change Ray Illingworth? Did he feel bitter, or did he mellow? Was the white rose chewed up by the running fox, or did the fox run faster on a diet of roses? Did the Yorkshireman of high principles impose his will on England cricket and its administration?

Ray's career has spanned three decades, from the days of the amateur into sponsorship and, who knows, to free collective bargaining. His skills as an all-rounder have been honed to a daily sharpness within their clear limitations.

Mike Stevenson, who played his own cricket for Staffordshire,

Cambridge University and Derbyshire, was party to the first decade and has observed the other two from fascinating vantage-points. First, as a schoolmaster in Pocklington he saw the youth of Yorkshire shape their traditional philosophies about cricket. Then, as a correspondent for the *Daily* and *Sunday Telegraph* and as a broadcaster, he has reported the day-to-day incident of County Cricket, mainly from the north.

In the press box he enthuses and argues his points with the authority of a divine conviction.

There will be times when Illingworth does not agree with Stevenson, and Stevenson with Illingworth — but that is what this book is all about, I hope, and that is why it is my pleasure to see how my two friends get on in the next couple of hundred pages.

TONY LEWIS

Introduction

When Raymond Illingworth left Yorkshire to join Leicestershire in 1969 at the age of thirty-seven, he had proved himself to be one of the finest county cricketers in the land; his Test Match record, however, was unimpressive. What was it that turned him, almost magically it seemed, into the man who brought back the Ashes and captained England so successfully in thirty-six Tests?

Opportunity to draw on his wealth of experience and native shrewdness as a captain transformed Leicestershire as it did England; under Illy they won the County Championship in 1975 for the first time in the club's history, twice won the Benson and Hedges Cup, in 1972 and 1975, and won the John Player Sunday League in 1974, three times finishing as runners-up in these competitions.

Which is his greatest accomplishment, the seventeen years with Yorkshire and the seven County Championships that he helped them to win, the great years as England's inspiration and leader or the remarkable revitalising of Leicestershire? If Illy's own view is correct that a test captain's task is generally easier than that of a county captain, then he would probably like to be judged on his record with Leicestershire; the faithful band of loyal Yorkshire nationalists will presume on the other hand that his greatest years in cricket still lie ahead; others will regard his appointment to the new post of team manager of Yorkshire from April 1979 as verging on demotion when compared with the climaxes of his career.

Illy is temperamentally incapable of looking backwards. He will hope that Geoff Boycott, whom he would have honoured with the vice-captaincy in Australia in 1970, will succeed Mike Brearley as England captain. Only a rash man would deny the strong possibility that Boycott and Illingworth will serve jointly in the not far distant future as England's captain and team manager.

Some of his formative years in the Yorkshire sides of the early 1950s were not happy ones; this great club can now be proud of having gone a long way towards achieving a régime, and consequently a general atmosphere, that combines a degree of tolerance and understanding with the traditional competitiveness bred of the old autocracy.

His roots are deep in Yorkshire. The front door of his house may carry a knocker in the shape of Leicestershire's emblem of a fox, but that house is still situated in Pudsey, not far from Farsley cricket club, where Illy learned the game in the hard, uncompromising school of the Bradford League; one of the club's sightscreens still in use was sawn, planed, sanded, joined, checked and painted by Fred Illingworth and his son almost thirty years ago when Illy was an apprentice joiner working for his father.

Situated between the two keenest cricketing cities in the world, Leeds and Bradford, Farsley has worn the passage of the years graciously. During one visit I saw an old man leading a cart horse up the main street while close by the dual carriageway that connects the two cities was heaving and stinking with a thousand cars.

The key to an understanding of Raymond Illingworth lies in the old Yorkshire and the rich vein of cricketing talent that the county knew it could mine; rebellion or failure by any player, however distinguished, merely meant that another of comparable ability would be called upon to occupy his place; a cricketer then would earn far more than his friends in mine or factory.

How different it is now. A county cricketer these days has, in the majority of cases, to make considerable sacrifices to play the game; pre-war Yorkshire players directed their belligerence towards opponents and often each other rather than the club. When the President or Chairman spoke, forelocks were dutifully touched and caps doffed respectfully.

Raymond Illingworth, perhaps more forcefully than any other modern cricketer, represents the meeting-point of the old and the new. As a player his attitude and mentality are akin to those of the likes of Emmot Robinson and Arthur Mitchell, yet his career has developed in the age of the media, big money in sport and of free collective bargaining.

1 The Walkabout

A soldier will reveal his true qualities in battle; he must not be judged on his conversation, his performance on the parade ground or even on the facility with which he recalls his experiences in memoirs or the media.

Raymond Illingworth's long and distinguished career has contained a number of battles, none more fierce than those of the 1970-1 tour of Australia during which he helped to regain the Ashes for England.

The first problem that faced him on this tour was to win over the mercurial and unpredictable John Snow. If he had failed in this aim through poor man management or any other cause the success of the tour as a whole would have been jeopardised.

During the MCC's first first-class match, which was against South Australia, the first incident occurred. The game was dead as a contest when South Australia's first innings reply to MCC's 451 for 9 declared reached 649 for 9 declared; but John Snow early in the innings had fielded with a lassitude that had turned singles into twos and twos into threes to the obvious irritation of his colleagues, especially the bowlers! Ray's answer was to summon him to the manager's room and, in David Clark's presence, say to him, 'If you weren't an intelligent man, you'd be on the boat home, I'm perfectly happy for you to get fit in your own time. I don't want you to rush up to bowl at full pace until you're ready. I shall be needing you in the Tests but there's one thing I won't have and that is messing about in the field, so that the other bowlers say, "If he can mess about, so can we." If that happens it won't be long before the whole side has gone. I hope you can see some sense in this.'

If Snow had taken offence or refused to see Illy's point, a situation could easily have developed from which England would have suffered. Snow's bowling was the single most vital factor in winning the Ashes. Thereafter Ray and John got on well on the

1

tour and, after a marked improvement in Snow's fielding the following day, Illy made a point of thanking him for his co-operation. It was during the same match that a tail-ender called McCarthy hit John Snow back over his head several times; at the team dinner in the evening Geoff Boycott and Ray charged him with a lack of pride in his own performance. 'Fred would have grabbed the ball and anyone who'd hit him over the top would have bloody well known about it!' But John Snow clearly did not share this view; he was always a man for the big occasion, a characteristic that cannot have escaped the attention of the Sussex members over the years!

After a depressingly mediocre start to the tour, the first Test at Brisbane and the second at Perth were both drawn; it was during this match that the trouble started. There was some bounce in the wicket and John Snow could, unlike any other bowler in the match or indeed the series, get the ball up chest high from just short of a length. Umpire Lou Rowan at once appeared to presume that, every time this happened, Snow had bowled a bouncer and made his opinion known to bowler and captain in no uncertain terms. Ray replied, 'They're not bouncers, Lou. He's got the ability to make it get up from just short of a length and you can't take that away from a fast bowler.' Rowan was adamant that they were bouncers and there the matter rested until the next delivery, which Snow pitched on bouncer length; and as the ball fizzed high over the batsman's head, he said to Rowan, 'That's a bloody bouncer!' War had been declared.

It flared most dramatically in the seventh Test. The extra match had been arranged following the total loss of the third Test at Melbourne to continuous rain.

England were one up in the series and with their leading bats-man, Geoff Boycott, absent through injury made a disastrous start; they were bowled out for 184, largely by O'Keeffe's and Jenner's wrist spin, Illy being top scorer with 42, so that Australia, after one of the stormiest sessions in Test cricket, led by 80 on the first innings. The fuse was ignited when Terry Jenner ducked into a short delivery from Snow, who was then officially warned by umpire Rowan. Again the crucial definition of what constituted a bouncer was lurking behind the argument and ill feeling. Both Snow and Illingworth rounded on Rowan and Illy, admittedly incensed by what he regarded as gross injustice, was seen on countless television sets wagging an angry finger at Rowan, apparently rebuking him in the most forceful terms. What he actually said, stressing the word 'one', was, 'He's only bowled one bouncer. You can't warn him for persistent short bowling.' Ray is still bitter that no one came to check what had actually occurred and that the incident was therefore incorrectly reported. Illy was clearly at fault because he did not manage to conceal his anger and frustration, but he faced a desperately difficult situation from the cricketing angle alone; Ray knew John Snow in his fury to be quite capable of bowling a real bouncer as he had done at Perth, and then of course he would not have been allowed to bowl again during the innings. Illingworth freely admits now that he did not at the time consider the question of diplomacy. As an international cricketer he presumed that an umpire in an England/Australia Test match would be of international standard; Rowan's handling of a potentially explosive situation which had, in Ray's view, been created by Rowan's initial error in interpreting the law caused him to flare up in the heat of the moment. Norman Tasker, a well-respected Australian sportswriter, said that 'if Lou Rowan and Ray Illingworth had been out West there'd have been gunplay'; but it was significant that Tasker came down squarely in Illingworth's defence. 'He was right. Snow was not bowling more than the occasional bouncer. What Rowan described as a bouncer was only just short of a length.'

Another cause of Illy's wrath was Rowan's claim that Snow had no right to bowl a bouncer to a tail-ender. Jenner had scored a century in a State match and was a competent bat; in the innings in question he was eventually fourth highest scorer for Australia with 30 at number ten. It was exceeding the legitimate powers of an umpire, he felt, for Rowan to make a pronouncement of this sort. What followed must be viewed against a background of intense personal resentment between Illingworth and Rowan and the former's belief that Rowan's actual umpiring had deteriorated from initial competence to a point at which an official letter of complaint to the Australian Board was written by Ray Illingworth which the manager, David Clark, refused to hand to the Board before the final Test was concluded.

After the angry exchanges between the three principal actors, Snow retired to long leg and the bombardment of bottles and cans soon commenced. There have been differing accounts of what followed, and Lou Rowan's own version in his book *The Umpire's Story* seems so transparently motivated by emotional involvement and personal prejudice that it is easier to trust, for example, the critical but generally fair and moderate description of events in E. W. Swanton's book, *Swanton in Australia*. In one important particular, however, Ray Illingworth is critical over an error of fact. 'Jim Swanton and one or two others got the incident wrong because they said that I took the side off the field the first time there was any trouble. That's completely wrong. It was the second time that there were cans and bottles thrown. After the first lot were thrown I called the players to the middle and we sat down for two or three minutes, while some cops came on and cleared them off. Then we started to walk to our places and the throwing started again. If Brooks and Rowan had taken charge and had made the right announcement to the crowd, for example, "Behave yourselves or there won't be any cricket to watch" then I would never have been put in the position I was.'

Another point in Lou Rowan's account of the incidents is that a high proportion of the words used by Illy in their heated exchanges on the field were obscenities. Ray admits that swear words were used but is adamant that Rowan's version of what occurred is grossly exaggerated. What really precipitated matters was that during the first outbreak of rioting the umpires appeared to do nothing about it, and Ray recalls that it struck him at the time as odd if not ludicrous that a man who could walk slowly to the boundary during an earlier Test to request a small boy whom nobody else had apparently noticed not to dangle his feet over the pickets could behave in highly explosive circumstance s with such lordly indifference.

As the bottle- and can-throwing intensified for the second time, Rowan's reaction was to say that it was both safe and proper to resume play; now Illy felt that he had no choice but to take his side off the field. Several former Australian captains,

Richie Benaud and Bobbie Simpson among them, who had seen the whole sorry sequence of incidents from the press-box or broadcasting point, were in full agreement with Illy's decision.

His thinking must to some degree have been based upon memories of the Port-of-Spain Test against West Indies in 1960 when he and his colleagues, several armed with stumps, walked off through a wildly-incensed rioting mob, seriously relieved to reach the comparative safety of the pavilion. On that occasion the whole day's play had been lost while litter, bottles and cans had been cleared. When Illy took his side off at Sydney the time lost was under fifteen minutes. His only error was in failing to notify the umpires of his intention, a fact that he now regrets. Rioting through national bias combined with dangerously heavy drinking has become a sadly frequent ingredient of international sport. Illy's view is that his handling of the situation was right in essence; whether one looks to the east or the west for a comparable set of circumstances, the actual time lost over the whole affair, including toing-and-froing and discussion of the legalities, seems to support his opinion. It was unfortunate that he did not, in the hearing of the batsmen and a couple of senior England players, call upon Rowan and Brooks to act decisively and if they had not done so, then notify them of his intention to take his side off. If this had been done, the question of England forfeiting the match would not have arisen.

When the sides got back to playing cricket, Australia were eventually dismissed for 264, and a solid second-innings team effort in the absence of England's leading batsman, Boycott, set Australia 223 for victory on a wicket that was slightly sympathetic to spin. Even so John Snow was the man the Aussies feared and, after yorking Ken Eastwood, opening in place of Bill Lawry, who had been deposed as captain by Ian Chappell and dropped from the side, he misjudged a hook by Stackpole off Lever and badly dislocated a finger in the boundary fence in almost the exact spot where earlier his confrontation with the crowd had precipitated the troubles. Now Australia, with the cutting edge of the England attack crucially blunted by Snow's departure, were clear favourites.

A captain and a team must be judged in adversity, and agree-

5

ment is virtually universal that Illingworth's side, consistently frustrated by injury throughout the tour, responded superbly. Lever and Underwood chipped away at the early batting while Stackpole suggested that he was perfectly capable of winning the match single-handed; but Illy embarked upon one of the most vital and excellent bowling stints of his career. He dismissed Redpath and schemed out Walters, who, visibly vulnerable to speed, steered a delivery from Bob Willis with vertical bat to be caught by Basil D'Oliveira at third man. Now Greg Chappell and Ken Stockpole stood between England and the Ashes and Illy had them both, the former stumped and the latter bowled off his pads, sweeping. When the last wicket fell, Ray had earned figures of 3 for 39 off 20 eight-ball overs, easily England's best second-innings return. Fulfilment and a sense of achievement, even triumph, were in abundance. England had regained the Ashes; but it was a tragedy for all concerned that such a wonderful match should have been marred by bitterness and controversy.

Illy, whose stock with his players could hardly have been higher, had demonstrated qualities during the series in general and the last Test in particular that had almost endeared him to the Australian cricketing public.

The sort of love/hate relationship that had developed was based on an understanding of his character and his attitudes to life and cricket. Illy was and is temperamentally far nearer to the average Australian than he is to the generations of amateur England captains who so often appeared to lack his fighting qualities. Stubbornness is closely allied to courage: the former may have sometimes led him into error but the latter has prevented his flinching in a crisis. The heat had been intense but he had not wanted to leave the kitchen.

2 Origins

Raymond Illingworth was born in Pudsey on 8 June 1932, in the house overlooking Pudsey church where his Aunt and Uncle live now, and his earliest recollection is of a set of stumps they gave him when he was only three. His parents, Fred and Ida, were very far from being rich folk, but the cabinet-making, joinery and furniture-polishing business that his father had worked to establish was beginning to show signs of real prosperity when the outbreak of war in 1939 caused the closing of the shop; it was sold when the war ended with Father employed at £12 per week in the business that he himself had developed, until the onset of chronic bronchitis cut short his working days.

It is more than likely that his father's experiences helped to mould Ray's acute awareness of the value of money; whether he is golfing for 50p, negotiating a contract or authorising extensive structural developments to his house, there is an essential solemnity about the transaction that was refined in the crucible of experience. Why should a man of talent spend his life working for others? Ability is marketable and must consequently be marketed.

Memories can sometimes be embarrassingly subjective, and Illingworth memories are no exception. He says that Dad was the disciplinarian of the family, but Mother, a frail but lively and spirited old lady (living in Bryan Street, Farsley at a weekly rent of £1.14!), recalls 'Father wasn't as strict as me.'

Mother remembers Raymond as 'a comical little chap, quiet but very shy, who'd have hid if you stopped to talk to anyone'.

Raymond got his first Sunday School prize when he was three. Whether or not orthodox, Nonconformist religion played a considerable role in the Illingworth household, there is no doubt that it contributed to forging the qualities which have made Yorkshiremen from Rockley to Don Wilson the redoubtable competitors that they have consistently proved themselves to be.

7

Talking to Mrs Illingworth was illuminating and instructive. Suffering had lined the strong features but the personality was unambiguous. Amidst talk of electricians, neighbours and current woes one memory obtruded with such vigour that it sought expression with a strength and spontaneity that contrasted with our quiet conversation. 'Once,' she said, 'when Raymond had more or less established himself in the Yorkshire side, he came home in a real fury. He'd been batting with Willie Watson and the captain had waved to them to get on with it. Now Willie Watson hadn't taken any notice but Raymond had done what he'd been told and got out and he was furious.'

Back down the corridor of the years had come rushing the memory of her son, called upon by authority to act in a certain way, obeying and suffering for it.

Mrs Illingworth was fiercely independent. 'We used to go to the Unitarians in Pudsey but I never managed to get on with the Baptists here in Farsley. They seemed a bit — well — different. A bit stuck-up. I've always been called Mrs Illingworth here and no one calls me Ida. At Pudsey everyone knew me. I was Ida to everyone.'

Geographical contiguity could not alter the apparently inescapable fact that Farsley was Farsley and Pudsey was Pudsey and between was a great gulf fixed.

At the age of three Ray and his parents emigrated to Farsley, where he later attended Frances Street School and recalls cricket in the playground. A teacher, Teddie Shepherd, having observed the inordinate monopolising of the batting time by the young Illingworth, used to purvey underhand leg-spinners and googlies in order to try to get some of the other lads the chance of a knock, but evidently Ray was no easier to dismiss at eight than in later years.

Fred, Illy's father, was a keen cricketer, but the summit of his attainment was Sunday School League cricket, the standard of which Ray believes was comparable to much of what he has seen of the Bradford League now and, although his grandfather was a bowls champion, one cannot glibly attribute to heredity the presence and development of an outstanding talent for sport.

Scouts from a number of famous clubs were interested in Ray's footballing ability, and his great friend Donald Jones was also a highly promising player; but there was not the financial reward in soccer that there is now and from an early age these two had set their sights on playing cricket for Yorkshire. Both attended the Wesley Street Elementary School where Donald was the fastest runner (with Ray always in second place!); the school played their home matches on the Farsley ground, and this brought them their first contact with the club. Natural progression meant that evenings were soon spent in endless, dedicated practice when they were not indulging in a form of the game known as 'little cricket', in which the bowler would stand about six yards from the batsman and the fielders crowd within inches. Slogging was taboo and the batsman was encouraged to keep every shot on the ground.

When the lads were not playing at the club they would be cricketing at the 'Wreck'. (The 'W' may sound odd if 'Wreck' were merely short for 'Recreation Ground', but as the purchase of seed and hours of work as groundsmen were required to keep it in trim perhaps the 'W' was justified.)

One element in school life that contrasts with the present day was discipline. Ray recalls the six-foot sticks with which the Headmaster, Mr Ingham, and his colleague Mr Sutcliffe were equipped, and it was well understood that if a boy or girl misbehaved a firm caning on hand or bottom would result. An unquestioning belief in the necessity for discipline (ideally self-imposed but failing that imposed from without) was one of the basic tenets that the young Illingworth acquired and has never lost. In this context he is thoroughly critical of the standard of discipline in schools today; he was not a tearaway and survived his school years without being caned. Clearly the Wesley Street authorities knew their man when he was put in charge of the checking and lodging of the National Savings money contributed by the children! This duty would only have been entrusted to a twelve-year-old boy who had demonstrated honesty and reliability (though members of the Yorkshire committee and of the TCCB may be forgiven a wry smile!).

Though he was certainly no roughneck, Illy was no angel. One day he was required to go with a friend to pick up a new cane for a teacher from a basket works, but when the dreaded object was first used it broke clean in two (doubtless to the relief of the recipient), having been sawn rather more than half way across in time-honoured fashion, to the general appreciation of all spectators.

It is another signpost towards an understanding of Ray Illingworth's credo to analyse his opinion on schools and teaching. 'In the old days, if a child misbehaved there was a smack coming and the child knew it. When our youngsters started at a school near here, a free-thinking school, a kid could take her work out and work in the hall. I just don't believe that any child under nine years old is capable of that. I think that when a child gets to fifteen or sixteen, she either wants to work or mess about and it's up to the individual. I think before that a child has to be made to get down to work whether she likes it or not.'

It is easy to over-emphasise the influences of childhood, but in Illy's case it seems certain enough that action and re-action contributed to a clear philosophy that might perturb the free-thinking liberal but is none the less a major formative influence in the growth of character and opinion. We live in an age of polarisation. Reactionaries become more reactionary because progressives seem to them to become progressively more divorced from reality. Recently, as reported in the national press, a teacher who instructed a member of his class to remove her coat was met with obscene defiance. On complaining to the headmaster, the teacher was rebuked for 'stirring things up' and the girl in question defended. Raymond and his headmaster would have danced *Swan Lake* together before it could have happened at Wesley Street.

Ray Illingworth was exceptionally shy as a boy and young man, a fact confirmed by his mother-in-law, Mrs Milnes, who recalls that he blushed scarlet every time she spoke to him. Sport is a great social lubricant, however, and it was through sport that the slender, brown-haired, high-shouldered lad with the keen eyes of the born competitor became a ring-leader; but the gang's sins were venial enough, their gravest offence being the time the local bobby caught them sledging down one of the main roads and hauled them off to the police station until the entire outfit was collected by worried parents.

The competitive element entered into the boys' cricket when they were still at the fruit-stealing stage; seeing the lads practising unobtrusively in a remote corner of the ground, Eddie Hargrave, then a playing member of the Farsley club, decided to do something about it. 'I used to keep going over and having a word with these boys and their natural talent for cricket was obvious. One night we had a practice for first teamers only on the square in preparation for a cup tie, but when we'd done I fetched the lads down and they batted and bowled. Eric Hargate, Donald Jones and Raymond would have been around thirteen. Donald especially looked a perfect batsman, even a bit ahead of Raymond then.

'It was after this that folks began to take notice. I got the lads together and they entered the Bradford Junior League. My own lad, Brian, played but he was younger than Raymond. Actually he scored for the first match and told me afterwards that the lads had made him fiddle the score book by adding on a few runs. Eric Hargate had said to him, "Go on. Give him four. He's not doing so well." '

'After a real struggle the club agreed to an official junior section so long as it didn't cost them any money, so we started off getting subscriptions. The matches were played on an evening mid-week and the lads won everything. They won the league at least three times in succession and five times while Raymond was playing for us, and he was a first teamer for several of those seasons. Now it wasn't the day when every Tom, Dick and Harry had a car. These lads had to get all over the district. I remember us going to East Bierley. I told my son to put his whites in. "There's sure to be someone doesn't get." But when we got there at ten past six there were eleven Farsley Juniors out on the field practising and it's a terribly awkward journey. They won the league year after year. I remember promising them a bag of chips each if they won a Derby match against Bowling Old Lane and after the match I was talking to the other manager and Raymond came to me and said, "Come on, we're all in the chip shop." He was waiting for his money.'

This should surprise no one who knows Ray. An offer had

been made. He and his team had fulfilled their part and logically the hour of reckoning followed. The essential qualities and characteristics of the mature County and Test player were already apparent in his early teens with the one exception that he had not at that stage discovered how cold and cruel a place the limelight in professional sport could be.

Eddie Hargrave was not the first person to spot the potential captain. Illy had led the school side but it was not long before Eddie stepped down from the captaincy/manager role that the rules of the League allowed and with prophetic insight entrusted the job to Ray. 'Raymond was always a mature lad but he'd listen to advice and he was never the least big-headed.'

Eddie had worked as a carding engineer in a wool mill and regularly took his tea and clothes to work to get changed and go straight to cricket from the mill. 'But I got that keen and involved it were worth it. I remember the Sunday morning after Raymond had played his first match for Yorkshire and he was up at the club playing "Little Cricket" with the lads, when the *Yorkshire Post* reporter came to interview him. He didn't find it too easy. It was "Come on Illy, it's your turn." Raymond told me that morning that he'd swung a ball from Cannings away to square-leg in the air, almost a six and the crowd had gone mad but Norman Yardley had come down tapping the wicket and said, "Keep 'em on the floor, lad." That's what's wrong with Yorkshire cricket.'

It is ironical that Eddie should have chosen for his disapproval one of the more gentle, liberal and least authoritarian of Yorkshire captains, but one still knows well what he means. The late Arthur Mitchell, whom Ray admired tremendously, would have spoken as Norman did, whereas Maurice Leyland (as indeed he once did in the county nets to Bryan Stott) would more likely have enquired if the unorthodox stroke in question yielded enough runs to make the risk taken a good investment. If the answer had been 'Yes' he would have said, 'Then keep playing it, lad.'

Eddie was critical of the way the club had initially viewed junior cricket before the success of the team had provided a flow of native talent as opposed to professionals and 'shamateurs' signed for the first team. In fact it was as a firm but gentle protest over the lack of encouragement given at all levels up to and including selection for the Bradford League side at Farsley that he curtailed his own playing days by premature retirement in order to concentrate on the juniors. Men like Eddie are close to the real bone and sinew of the game and in the case of Raymond Illingworth the gratitude he felt then and feels now is probably sufficient reward for the time, money and energy that Eddie unselfishly spent.

One last word from Eddie Hargrave. 'I can't claim to have really been a coach but I used to encourage the lads and if they made an error I used to make a note about it and have a word with them after the game. I remember Donald Jones used to get into a tangle with one that spun in to him and bowled him off his pads. Well, I couldn't bowl off-spinners so I took him away to a bit of sloping ground and bowled onto the slope so that the ball turned in to him.'

Not a coach indeed! He showed unobtrusive intelligence, a willingness to work practically with the young player in question and, above all, the flexibility of the born improviser. Many coaches who stand behind the net and just talk at their charges could learn from Eddie Hargrave.

3 'David and Jonathan'

Talk to any of the Farsley Cricket Club members and the name that always crops up alongside that of Raymond (never Ray!) Illingworth is that of Donald Jones. The two were inseparable. Both possessed outstanding sporting talent and fanatical dedication, but general opinion believed then that the better cricketing prospect of the two was Donald Jones. Both were selected for the club's first team before they were fifteen and it is significant that Ray still recalls vividly the boyhood opinion he held himself that Donald was the better player.

In one crucial respect, however, they could not have been more different. Donald's highly-strung temperament, which could sometimes make him physically ill before he went in to bat, contrasted starkly with Ray's infinitely more phlegmatic and matter-of-fact approach. Even while he was a junior, the tougher the situation the better the young Illingworth batted, and at this stage he was primarily a batsman, his effective medium-paced swing bowling coming largely as a bonus.

On one occasion an exciting century scored in quick time had put Ray in sight of the Bradford League record, achieved by W. Payton in 1919, but when Donald Jones joined him Ray was quite content to push singles in order to give his friend the strike, a fact that undoubtedly prevented the record being broken. Illy reserved his most spectacular exploit for a neighbouring club, Pudsey St Lawrence, for whom he might well have played. He scored 148 not out in a Priestley Cup match that occupied several evenings and attracted record attendance; the irony was that Illy had gone for trials with the Pudsey club and only opted to play for Farsley as a lad because they had chosen him instantly for the second team.

Until both Illy and Donald joined the RAF their careers ran side by side, a steady gradation from Farsley and the Bradford League through the Yorkshire Federation to the Colts. Donald

15

recalls the early days when their gang, with Ray's father Fred in attendance, walked the three miles to Calverley Park, taking with them a large roller and mower. There they cut and rolled a wicket before holding a full-scale match with Fred as umpire. On another occasion the Illingworths took Donald to Bridlington, where the arrival of the first meal of the holiday caused the forth-right Fred to announce to the boarding-house-keeper, 'Tha'd better bring t'lads same again, Missus. They can't play cricket on that!'

Memory is still vivid of the day that Len Hutton came to see Farsley's two promising young players at the nets, and doubt-less his gift of a bat to each was doubly welcome. On the Federation tour Donald Jones' father returned the Illingworths' kindness by curing Ray's travel sickness through the simple expedient of making him sit on a newspaper, a curious form of treatment that proved surprisingly effective. Brian Close and Fred Trueman were also on this tour, and Donald remembers the then slender, black-avised Fred, attired in a black belt, bowl-ing slow, left hand before the match and very fast right hand during it, to the embarrassment of the Sussex side, who soon found themselves five wickets down without scoring.

Both the lads were tremendous fans of Arthur Mitchell, who coached them at the county nets, and it is no exaggeration to say that when the time came for their period of compulsory National Service the future was beginning to beckon alluringly. Donald was posted to Kirkham in Lancashire and, having requested his commanding officer permission to leave half an hour early on a Saturday to make it possible for him to play Bradford League cricket, was summarily refused: 'You've not joined the RAF to play cricket, Jones!'

And that in effect was that. He married during his time in the services and relinquished all ideas of professional sport, which he regarded as too risky a career for a married man; those who knew his promise and talent as a lad regarded the clean break he made with cricket as a considerable loss to the game. Over twenty years later he is sane and realistic enough to see his decision in the clearest perspective. 'I suppose I could have tried proing in the Bradford League but I'd probably have made about fifty bob a match. Even the county players were only getting around twenty pounds a week. People like Raymond and Doug Padgett, magnificent cricketers, were near the breadline when they were with Yorkshire in the early days. I just wasn't prepared to take the risk. The only regret is that I didn't find out whether or not I could have made it.'

Now Donald Jones is a representative for Wilson Steel Services and his wife runs a dress shop in Ilkley. They are comfortably off and their house, almost on the banks of the river in Burley-in-Wharfedale, is 'a highly desirable residence'. But that little nagging question will always probe unobtrusively in Donald's mind: 'Did I do the right thing or did Raymond?'

Ray's RAF career could hardly have been more opposed to that of his boyhood friend. He was called up in October 1950 and was initially posted to Cheltenham, where he met a cricketing officer sufficiently interested in his talent and promise to see that he was swiftly shuttled back to Dishforth in Yorkshire. Near-disaster followed; an acute attack of pneumonia was diagnosed as fibrositis. He was given oxygen *en route* for the Military Hospital in York where he was on the danger list for some time. His mother remembers that during and after his illness 'he looked like a little old man'. It needed considerable collective family determination to prevent an operation being performed that would have removed part of the rib cage and almost certainly impaired his chances of success as a bowler.

But that illness was the only set-back. RAF Dishforth is only thirty miles from Bradford and his duties in the PTI stores were not unduly taxing; one of his most cherished memories is managing to complete his stint of service without actually performing guard duty! Cricket there was in abundance — for Farsley, Yorkshire Colts, the RAF and the Combined Services. This period of Services cricket was an important formative influence on Illy and a number of Yorkshire and other county players. Other Yorkshiremen who played for the Services around this time were Brian Close, Fred Trueman, Bryan Stott, Philip Sharpe and Bob Platt, who had this to say about Combined Services cricket and his captain, Squadron-Leader Alan Shirreff: 'For county and second team players, the couple of years spent in Services' cricket with Alan were better than anything a county could offer. A bad day was quickly forgotten, though we did have very interesting *post mortems* at dinner, where we ate as a team irrespective of rank.'

The point was surely that, however seriously this cricket was conducted, the ultimate pressure of competing with and against fellow professionals in the county set-up was eased for a time, and so development of latent talent could be more natural and spontaneous.

This opportunity was perhaps especially crucial to a young cricketer like Ray brought up in the taxing arena of the Bradford League and the Colts. He played against Ken Earl of Northumberland, then appreciably the fastest bowler in the country, and at the age of seventeen just managed to prevent the bat being knocked out of his hand. Earl was narrowly pipped for selection for the 1950-1 MCC tour of Australia under Freddie Brown by John Warr, a fine county bowler in English conditions but one who was unable to pass the stern examination of test cricket in Australia. Ray believes that professional selectors would unhesitatingly have given their vote to Earl, not Warr. (Had they done so, the tourists would have been deprived of a colleague who may have earned the unenviable figures of 1 for 281 in his two tests against Australia, but nevertheless contributed similar qualities to those of Morecambe and Wise!)

Illy's first real success at top level was the occasion of his début for the county on 18 August 1951. He had been selected for Combined Services against Warwickshire when the cry for aid came from the Yorkshire authorities. Having been released by the Services, Ray reported to Headingley, where the skill and hostility of that fine new ball bowler, Vic Cannings of Hampshire, had accounted for four good Yorkshiremen and true; Harry Halliday, Ted Lester, Vic Wilson and Billy Sutcliffe had all been clean bowled when Raymond Illingworth came out to join his captain, Norman Yardley, in his first innings for the greatest cricket club in the world.

Cannings could be a handful with his late outswing and his ability to cut the ball off the seam, so that Ray's fifty-six out of a hundred stand with Yardley represented a personal triumph as

well as initial evidence of a stalwart character equipped to face
adversity. Although Farsley was technically included in the
borough of Pudsey at that time, Farsley folk who read *Wisden*
cannot have been enamoured with the immortalising of this
splendid knock in these words: 'Yardley received fine assistance
from Illingworth, a nineteen-year-old all-rounder from Pudsey
making his first county appearance. Illingworth showed the right
temperament and good stroke-play. His cover-driving was of the
best quality.' When one recalls the melancholy fact that on his
début at Fenner's Fred Trueman was described as 'a spin
bowler' it would be ungracious to condemn Wisden for
presuming that Ray's cricketing loyalties were firmly attached to
his birthplace.

One other highly significant development in his career had
already taken place by this time. It was to have far-reaching
results. As long ago as his Wesley Street schooldays, Illy recalls
bowling his medium pace in a match against another school and
suddenly slipping in an off-spinner that turned appreciably, an
occurrence that prompted the visiting umpire to admonish him
for 'wasting your time with medium pace when you can spin the
ball like that'. The advice which fell on deaf ears then was
heeded a year or two later. From time to time he would experiment with spinners at the Farsley nets. This had been duly noted
by Jackie Firth, later to become Leicestershire's cheerful and
efficient wicket-keeper. During a match at Saltaire in which
Farsley were dismissed on a rain-affected wicket for a meagre
fifty-eight, Jack, noting that the accredited Farsley spinners were
largely ineffective, said to Ray, 'You can bowl better bloody
spinners than this. Get yourself on and give it a go.' The result
was a spectacular return of five wickets for five runs and
unpredictable victory for Farsley by three runs.

The changed style was also noted at the county nets by Messrs
Bowes and Mitchell, who had privately felt that Ray lacked a
yard or two of pace to meet Yorkshire's needs as a seamer, and
official approval was granted. From the day of that remarkable
match Illy underwent instant transformation and though he
occasionally bowled seamers for Yorkshire (actually taking as
many as forty first-class wickets in a season by this method) he

became and was to remain an off-spinner whose skill, accuracy and shrewdness may even have contributed to his batting being to some degree under-rated if not actually neglected. Apart from a short spell as opener with Frank Lowson, Ken Taylor or Brian Close he spent more time at number seven than anywhere else, though he was regularly promoted and demoted up and down the batting order.

When his period of National Service ended he returned to his father's joinery business with something less than enthusiasm; ever since leaving school at the age of fourteen (the school-leaving age was increased to fifteen the following year) Ray had worked for his father when the demands of cricket and football would allow. He was a fair craftsman though it is not unkind to suggest that his heart was not in the job. Eddie Hargrave remembers the Illingworths, father and son, coming to his house to polish a suite of furniture: 'Raymond spent the time staring out of the window.' (The other side of the coin is the attractive bedroom furniture, made with his own hands, adorning his daughter's room in their house in Farsley, also the sight-screen referred to in the introduction, still in use at Farsley cricket club, that he and Fred made together when Ray was 'nobbut a lad'.)

Now the slender boy who had made Pudsey St Lawrence suffer in the Priestley Cup was fast maturing into wiry athleticism. Sam Blackburn's coaching at Wesley Street, the runs over Stanningley Fields to the lads' favourite cinema, called the Pudsey 'New Un' (when he and Donald Jones could, if they were lucky, outdistance the little red bus known as the 'Farsley Flier' as well as save the fare!), the long golden evenings of boyhood, endlessly and tirelessly cricketing, were beginning to recede in his memory; but he has never forgotten.

Raymond Illingworth, even more than most of us, is a product of home and school where he learned the value of discipline as well as the value of money; perhaps above all, he is the product of an area and an ethos where the game of cricket provides opportunity of expression to dour, rugged but often warm and lovable people who see in it a challenge, a testing-ground for courage and tenacity and above all that need for the creative fulfilment that the poet finds in verse and the singer in his song.

4 The Greatest Club in The World?

Man, we are told by the sage, is a social animal. The more primitive the society, the more closely knit it can be and there is something primitive (if not primeval!) in the Yorkshire County Cricket Club. The waves of change rolled and broke about its tall cliffs but for years it survived in essence unaltered from its pre-Second World War régime.

The paternalistic role that Lord Hawke played is too well known to warrant restatement or development here. 'Pray God no professional shall ever captain England,' said his Lordship, and to those who diagnose in this pronouncement ultimate, unforgiveable snobbery a word of caution. Before cricket moves irreversibly towards the attitudes and atmosphere of Association Football, the debt that cricket owes to the disinterested, independent amateur captain must be acknowledged, though clearly the country's economic and social background was hugely different when the amateur captain flourished. (The story may be apocryphal that the Hon. F. S. Jackson declined an invitation to play in a Test Match in order to attend a day's grouse shooting. If it is not true it ought to be!)

Nobody in his right mind can object to the present collective description of the game's players as 'cricketers', as opposed to the divisive 'amateurs' and 'professionals', but real enterprise and independence are all too rarely discovered in the captains of today. Yorkshire owes gratitude to the generations of amateurs who, at worst, were figureheads manipulated by the great players under them but at best provided the discipline and unity of purpose necessary to weld the combative, assertive, demanding characters in their charge into an effective fighting unit. Even the less forceful captains could ultimately represent the authority of the club more effectively than could any world-famous gladiator.

21

The Yorkshire County Cricket Club it seemed (many would substitute the present tense!), like any Victorian or Edwardian family, needed a patriarch, and in the year that Ray Illingworth was born the predestined successor to Lord Hawke, Brian Sellers, played his first match for Yorkshire.

During the 1920s Yorkshire's grip had tightened with four successive Championships and they had never fallen below fourth; George Hirst retired in 1921 after a playing career of thirty-two years, while his friend and colleague Wilfred Rhodes continued to torment batsmen and bowlers alike until his fifty-third year, after a similar span. They were giants and to club cricketers now who have consigned themselves to a geriatric role in the game represent, according to the temperament of the individual, the ultimate encouragement or condemnation. Yorkshire won the Championship every year from 1922 to 1925. Yorkshire lost only six matches out of 122 and incredibly half of their victories were by an innings. Some believe that the sides of the early 1920s were the greatest ever to represent the county.

This was one of the great eras of the club. It is difficult to compare it with the superb sides of the 1930s when Yorkshire would probably have brushed aside with contemptuous ease a considerable number of the alleged Test teams to emerge in recent years. The fact that they failed to win the Championship in 1934 and 1936 (though they triumphed in seven of the nine seasons prior to the suspension of cricket at the close of the 1939 season) suggests that the overall standard of the county game was far higher than it is today.

Despite the inexaggerable skill and competitive appetite of Sutcliffe, Leyland, Hutton, Bowes and Verity it could be convincingly argued that the key figure was Brian Sellers. 'The Crackerjack', as he was known, managed to establish and maintain the relationship with his opponents and victims that was enjoyed by Drake and Frobisher in Elizabethan times. To admirers and well-wishers he was a combination of hero and Messiah — to critics, a predator and a pirate.

The essential character of Yorkshire cricket in the post-war years was fashioned by that of the 1920s and 1930s, when Sellers brought to his task as Yorkshire captain the religious intensity of those Puritans who rode into battle inspired by a banner bearing the legend 'Christ and no quarter'. When Illy was a boy, Yorkshire were winning by an innings and grinding the opposition into the Headingley and Park Avenue turf.

This bred a legacy of admiration mingled with resentment if not actual hatred. I vividly recall the apparent bitterness evinced against Yorkshire by the other counties with whom I contended as a struggling undergraduate cricketer at Cambridge. When one played against Yorkshire there was an edge, a feeling of being hunted; it was as if one were being psychologically intimidated. The genuine courtesy, chivalry even, of a George Hirst, David Denton, Maurice Leyland, Cyril Turner or Norman Yardley were in stark contrast with the more typical view parodied (whether or not he ever uttered the words) in Wilfred Rhodes' 'we don't play this game for fun' and with the awareness of any Yorkshire wrist-spinner that he can expect short shrift in the county that bred Rhodes, Verity, Wardle, Appleyard and Illingworth. ('We want you to take wickets, lad, but we can't see our way to letting you buy them!')

The sort of fiercely biased, passionate pride that characterised Yorkshire cricket in the 1920s and 1930s can bring the best and the worst out of people. Certainly there was no room for the 'star'. Herbert Sutcliffe may have felt privately that there was a degree of injustice in the fact that, as a world-class batsman of twenty years' service, he received the same remuneration as lesser mortals, but such thoughts were only uttered behind closed doors.

When war ended and cricket recommenced in 1946, Brian Sellers brought to his task of remoulding Yorkshire cricket the same unselfish dedication he had shown in the 1930s; Bill Bowes recalls how he used to say to him, 'We must keep at it, Bill, until Yorkshire have a side again.' In fact they had a side immediately but it was squarely based on the old guard. When Illy played truant with a couple of pals to see Yorkshire beat the Indians by an innings and eighty-two runs at Park Avenue in 1946, Len Hutton contributed 183 not out; Arthur Booth, tried by the county in 1931 and pipped for the regular slow left-arm position by the great Hedley Verity, claimed match figures of 10 for 91, ending the season head of the Yorkshire and of the national bowling averages in his forty-fourth year.

A quaint sequel to this truancy occurred in the form of a photograph in the *Yorkshire Evening Post* of the three evildoers, smiling happily at the head of the queue to enter Park Avenue, though whether the smiles were still prominent on entry into their headmaster's study is not recorded.

Wisden said of this 1946 season, perhaps a little naïvely, 'Under the leadership of Brian Sellers, the team, as in each summer from 1932, played with the zest and determination to win peculiar to Yorkshiremen. So well versed were they in the fighting spirit that when representative fixtures called away their best men, and sometimes the captain fulfilling his duties as a member of the Test Match selection committee, ability came to the front in such refreshing style that Yorkshire, true to themselves for so many years from the time when Lord Hawke became captain, invariably produced the man wanted at a moment's notice.' The point of course was that there were then so many fine cricketers in Yorkshire, many of whom were 'born to blush unseen' at first-class level that the surprising thing would have been if 'the man wanted at a moment's notice' had not been readily forthcoming.

Gradually after the triumphs of 1946 the pre-war players bowed out until, after the departure of Ellis Robinson to Somerset at the end of the 1949 season, only Norman Yardley, who had taken over the captaincy from Brian Sellers in 1948, and Len Hutton remained. Life, moreover, had not stood still while the Yorkshire side had been changing. Sellers was not, it seemed, too sad to retire and, writing in *Wisden* of 1948, he uttered a warning note. 'What I have seen of the average young player today as regards fielding ability rather shakes me. He does not seem to spend a great deal of time practising fielding, which is a thousand pities.' As so often, what remains unsaid is of greater importance than the overt meaning. He felt, I believe, that the long, hard, demanding apprenticeship that Yorkshire players had undergone before the war, demanding absolute obedience to club and captain and a high degree of dedication and self-discipline, were dwindling as fast as wartime memories;

social barriers and distinctions were becoming blurred. Privilege or alleged privilege was hunted and assailed. The bloodless revolution that was to lead to a vast redistribution of wealth and influence in our society was under way.

All these factors and many more contributed to the atmosphere and quality of the Yorkshire dressing-room when Ray Illingworth first became a member of the side; above all, the forceful, uncompromising Sellers had been succeeded as captain by the infinitely more gentle and relaxed Yardley.

He inherited a side that was no longer sufficiently powerful to trample on all but a few counties. Injury, illness and absence through National Service of key players presented further problems, so that Yardley's natural instinct to play a more adventurous game than had been traditionally associated with Yorkshire accelerated modification of the old ways. In his own words, 'As far as I was concerned, I was prepared to have a go at anything in county cricket. If you lose a match it doesn't really matter but it's different in a Test Match, where a great number of folks think it does matter. One's approach is bound to be different in a five-day Test to a three-day county match. You see, the Yorkshire side just was not good enough to roll them in the mud as we'd done before the war, so we had to make fancy declarations and try to pull in a few points from nowhere.'

But Yorkshire possessed the services of the world's greatest batsman, Len Hutton, who had made the gift of a cricket bat to a promising youngster from Farsley called Raymond Illingworth; in return Illy had sat goggle-eyed with admiration while Hutton plundered those 183 graceful runs from the Indians at Bradford and had ever since worshipped the ground over which Hutton's dancer's feet had twinkled.

When Ray won his place in the Yorkshire side, Brian Sellers, perhaps the most respected and admired captain in the county's history, was on the committee and soon to become its chairman and Norman Yardley, a transparently likeable man and a fine cricketer, was its captain. Surely no young cricketer could commence his career with better auguries or in more auspicious circumstances?

5 Baptism By Fire

Following Illy's triumphant initiation into county cricket in 1951, the next season saw him tally only four championship appearances scoring thirty-eight runs and capturing a modest four wickets. But the cricket he played in the services was keen and demanding.

His routine duties were not, and it is clear that a much more confident and less vulnerable young man, who had acquired the services' philosophy of expediency and unobtrusive application of Parkinson's Law, took his place in 1953 alongside ten colleagues who had played or were to play for England. The cold splash he experienced was largely owing to Bob Appleyard's illness, Fred Trueman's National Service and Brian Close's football injury, the result being a taxingly busy summer for himself and Johnny Wardle, who carried the Yorkshire attack.

Ray, apart from a highly creditable showing with the bat, bowled well over seven hundred championship overs, almost two hundred more than any Yorkshire bowler other than Wardle. It was not a gentle initiation and when one also considers the physical and mental strain inherent in three-day Championship cricket, especially for a newcomer, it is possible that these early experiences combined with native caution to result in periodic unwillingness to over-expose himself in the firing-line when conditions were unfavourable to his craft.

Critics may spit, 'Rubbish! Ray is and has always been a selfish cricketer. There's no more to it than that.' I honestly cannot agree. He has never been a selfish batsman and his thinking generally has surely been based on the old cricketing concept that a dedicated player will, nine times out of ten, serve his side best by appearing to serve himself. It is that tenth time that is so significant and in this context Illy's record as a batsman is commendable, while his record of overs bowled and wickets taken for Yorkshire speaks for itself. (He may also have remembered that

Donald Waterhouse, a superb medium-pacer for Farsley who was also their captain in several of Ray's formative years consistently over-bowled himself.)

Early in May at Hull, Yorkshire lost five wickets for a hundred and four runs to Bailey, Smith and Greensmith of Essex before Illy joined his captain, as he had done at Leeds two years previously, with Yorkshire deep in trouble. On this occasion the junior cricketer was the senior partner. Cover-driving freely and fiercely, Ray plundered an exhilarating 146 not out, in helping his side to 366 for 7 declared. Sober and reliable judges were forced dangerously close to the employment of superlatives but Dame Wisden, in her all-seeing majesty, confined her remarks to a cautious and factual, 'Illingworth played a leading part in Yorkshire's first innings recovery. He batted four and a quarter hours for his first century. Yardley helped him to put on 146 and Brennan stayed while 115 were added.' Jim Kilburn wrote in the *Yorkshire Post*, 'His off-driving was firm and eager and he swung cheerfully at anything outside his leg stump', a clear commentary upon a young player whose uninhibited attacking potential had not been cramped by the coming plethora of in-swing and in-slant bowling or a cautious desire to eliminate error through the avoidance of risk.

Norman Yardley still regarded Ray primarily as a batsman who could also bowl; he got his fair share of bowling but rarely used to get on before third or even fourth change, though 7 for 22 against Hampshire at Bournemouth in August and 6 for 29 against Kent at Dover, earlier the same month, provided salutary reminder of his effectiveness in favourable conditions; but despite an auspicious first full season for the young Illingworth, 1953 was far from a happy year for Yorkshire.

His admiration for the great Len Hutton as a batsman had not diminished, but certain of his attitudes jarred on a young player. On one occasion a journalist whom Illy liked and respected asked him in Hutton's hearing if the ball had been turning appreciably during an innings in which Ray had only managed to take a single wicket, admittedly at modest cost. He replied that the ball had been turning, only to be firmly contradicted by Len Hutton, who, after the journalist had left, instructed him firmly never to admit 'that the ball had turned if you've only managed to take one wicket'. It was felt, moreover, that Hutton's great store of knowledge and expertise should have been more readily made available to the young players, Ray among them, who admired and respected his great ability; but in this context it must be said in Len Hutton's defence that, rightly or wrongly, he was a staunch adherent of the Arthur Mitchell philosophy that presumed the need for a young cricketer to think things out for himself: to apply the most rigorous self-criticism and to expect from his peers and seniors in his moments of greatest triumph adverse comment upon the slightest flaw that might have prevented his success and therefore that of his side being even more complete. Hedley Verity would have sympathised; during his first season in the Yorkshire side he took 7 for 26 (also against Hampshire at Bournemouth) only to be told by his self-appointed guardian and tutor, Emmott Robinson, 'You let one slip down t'leg side, long-'op it were. Tha should have 'ad 7 for 22. Keep 'em up whatever you do.'

Irrespective of the rights and wrongs, Illy's disillusionment with Norman Yardley's leadership was as complete as in the case of his former idol, Len Hutton; undoubtedly Yardley had to deal with two tough and sometimes awkward characters in Johnny Wardle and Bop Appleyard, the latter returning to the side after prolonged illness in 1954. He headed the county bowling averages and helped to challenge Surrey's apparent invincibility, leaving Yorkshire runners-up at the season's close.

But it was common knowledge that the Yorkshire dressing room was far from a happy place. Len Hutton, who as senior professional could and should have been a calming influence in supplementing the captain's authority, seemed more intent to young Illy on fanning the flames of controversy; but the largest irritant came on the field, where Wardle and Appleyard seemed able to choose when, for how long and at which end to bowl, without concern for their colleagues or indeed the gentle decrees of their captain.

On numerous occasions Illingworth would be asked to bowl by Yardley and on presenting himself at the wicket would be told by one or other of his tormentors, 'Bugger off! I'm bowling here'; to his chagrin and amazement absolutely nothing would be done about it. It would be hard to imagine anything more detrimental to team spirit or indeed a young player's enthusiasm. Wardle, moreover, interspersing as he often did the chinaman or left-hander's off- break with his orthodox slow, leg breaks, used to demand and get the end which Ray, owing to slope or breeze, thought natural for his off-spin. Slights and pinpricks like these were surely the origin of a keen sense of grievance that has caused him to be branded by his critics, and even smilingly by his friends, as a moaner; but in his early days in the Yorkshire side, he had a good deal to moan about, though he also possessed a tendency towards the neurotic, exemplified by the plaintive theory expressed to a member of the press that 'he's had me on at the wrong end. The wind's been blowing the spin off the ball.'

To anyone as shrewd, calculating, efficient and accustomed to meticulous planning of every move on and off the field as Illy, the régime in these early years in the 1950s must have been frustrating and infuriating in the extreme. It is easy to understand why Wardle and Appleyard were as they were, but understanding is not exoneration. It was thought wise by the Yorkshire establishment to encourage the feeling that there were others breathing down a player's neck and ready to take his place if he should falter. It was not just bravery and dedication that prompted Jimmie Binks, who would not stand down even with badly bruised or broken fingers, to play 412 consecutive matches for Yorkshire, 123 more than any other county keeper; he was influenced by a genuine desire to hold on to what he had. Doubtless Wardle and Appleyard felt the same. Woe betide anyone who dropped a catch off their bowling. The skies would darken and the thunder roll. Again it was the youngsters who suffered most and a marked falling-off in the standard of fielding predictably resulted. Roy Booth, later to join Worcestershire, reached the sad stage that he was virtually unable to keep wicket to Johnny Wardle and during a match at Hull, when Mike Cowan dropped a catch off Wardle at mid-off and apologised, the snarled reply came back: 'It's my own bloody fault for putting you there'. Wardle had his arm round Cowan as he spoke so that anyone watching the incident from a distance would have presumed he was speaking sympathetically.

A good fielder normally prays that the ball will be hit to him. He does not enjoy being out of the game and it is a sorry state of affairs that virtually guarantees failure if a player is muttering to himself, 'Please God, don't let him hit it to me.' The moment of truth as far as Illy was concerned came after he too had started to pray for the ball not to come to him. Eventually the inevitable happened and he dropped a catch off Wardle's bowling. When taken to task by the incensed bowler, Ray's natural inhibitions flew out of the dressing-room window and a real shouting match ensued. 'I told him I'd always been a good fielder, which I had been in the Bradford League, and I could catch as well as anyone else. The reason I was missing them was his bloody attitude to everybody and I remember Johnny saying, "Don't you take it like that. I thought we got on well." I said, "What other way can I take it and what's happening to the whole bloody side? As far as I'm concerned you can get stuffed. I've been a good fielder and I'll be a good fielder again if you'll only leave people alone." From then on I'd no problem. I'd got it off my chest and out of the way. After that when anyone was slogging, Johnny used to put me where they were hitting and the following year I copped thirty-three catches in the outfield.'

Another significant little glimpse of the Yorkshire side in the mid-1950s is provided by the words 'Johnny used to put me where they were hitting.' Strange that it appeared then to be the duty of the bowler and not the captain to place the field.

As unmistakable as in the case of a Trueman or a Boycott the Pennine gritstone was being carved by the wind and weather of experience into the shape that we know now. Illy is a tolerably resilient character. His attitudes were modified but he survived this harsh apprenticeship. A more vulnerable person might not have been so fortunate and, in fact, when I asked Frank Lowson, one of the finest post-war batsmen Yorkshire has produced, to help me in a previous project on Yorkshire cricket, he declined, 'I'd like to help you but honestly I just don't want to think about those days.'

Illingworth's great boyhood god, Len Hutton, had proved in his eyes to have feet of clay and Norman Yardley, though he had never forfeited his liking as a man, had lost Ray's respect as a captain through turning his back on everyday problems of man-management as if they did not exist.

Of the three major figures mentioned at the close of the pre-ceding chapter, Brian Sellers remains. Sellers was unquestion-ably a great captain and great captains are as rare as chuckles in a mausoleum; but the very qualities that had contributed to his leadership, namely physical courage, unselfish dedication to Yorkshire cricket, blunt, at times crude and even brutal frank-ness of speech and the distinctive brand of Yorkshire nationalism ('He's good enough to play for England but not for Yorkshire'!), were apparently grafted onto his duties as an administrator, as if the problems and responsibilities of a captain were exactly similar to those of the chairman of the cricket committee. Con-frontation was inevitable.

Talking to Illy now of those daunting days in the 1950s, one is struck by the obvious influence they exerted on his credo of leadership. Speaking with the hindsight of the Leicestershire and England captaincy and the maturity the intervening years have bestowed, he has no doubt as to how the situation should have been handled. 'I would have hoped to have handled things well enough to avoid them getting to the situation we had. Above all there had to be one boss and that's the captain. If a bowler tried to take himself off or keep himself on against what I'd said, his feet wouldn't have touched the ground. To start with I'd have had a word with, say, Bob Appleyard and told him that it was my job to make the decisions. If I'd put someone on to bowl then he would bowl and if, after a couple of warnings, he'd done it again and challenged my authority, then the only thing left to do would be to go to the committee and say, "Either he goes or I go." That would be the ultimate but I'd have fought and fought to prevent it getting to that stage.'

Any captain who surrenders his authority must surely invite the disintegration of his side. One can still register nostalgic sympathy for Norman Yardley. The real conflict (excluding per-sonalities for a moment) was cricket played essentially for enjoy-ment and cricket as a job of work. If Norman had captained Yorkshire in the 1930s he would probably have experienced the same problems. Yorkshire needed a Sellers in the 1950s and the crowning irony is that he was then in a position in which those qualities most admirable in a captain guaranteed friction and resentment in an administrator. Practically without exception those who played under him described Norman Yardley as 'too nice a man to be a good captain', which is in no sense intended as a criticism of his knowledge of tactics or of the game generally. This judgement tells us at least as much about several of the players under him as it does about their captain.

In addition the régime must bear its full share of the blame. The bowler hat and rolled umbrella image of the autocrat demanding total dependence and absolute subservience may have been exaggerated in the minds of Yorkshire cricketers, but it clearly influenced their thinking in the difficult time of transition from the paternalism of the old days to the new independence. The Yorkshire committee was fighting according to its lights to maintain the standards of service and loyalty on which past success had been based. Surely, as so often happens, the pendulum has swung too far.

6 'To See Oursels as Others See Us'

Ray Illingworth's talent as a cricketer is not in question; nor is the convincing image projected by television and radio that decreasing shyness and increasing articulacy have created. These constitute the appearance of a famous man. What is the reality?

Three contemporaries who knew, as Illy did, the good times and the bad can help to answer this question. The first is the county's present coach, Doug Padgett, who, making his début for Yorkshire in 1951 at the age of sixteen, the same year as Illy, was the youngest cricketer ever to play for Yorkshire.

Doug shares with his predecessor, the late Arthur Mitchell, extreme care in the weighing of every word. Pauses are long, meditation profound. Arthur was once questioned about some technical point concerning bowling, to which he replied, after milking a stupendous pause, 'Bowlers? Bowlers? [another long pause] Aye, bowlers. They're something no side should be without.'

Doug Padgett would not admit that Ray had changed at all in the long years since they met in the late 1940s. 'He's always been logical and thoughtful. Everything he did, he'd map it out. We were both very young when we started so we tended to keep our mouths shut and try to learn from people who were household names to us. There was the aggro and as a lad you didn't much want to drop a catch at twenty to twelve and be out there for the rest of the day, being reminded of it. After the days when Raymond was a batsman who could bowl seamers a bit, he still didn't get on all that much, as Appleyard and Close would get on before him with off-spinners. If you asked him in those days, "When do you bowl?", a typical answer would be, "When the bloody ball isn't turning." His job was bowling length and line. When we used to bowl spinners in championship cricket,

Wardle used to say many a time, "Bowl tight for half-an-hour. Keep it tight and I'll do the same." You might not know where a wicket would ever come from but someone would play an indiscriminate shot and get out; but if someone bowled a long hop or a full toss it eased the tension and everything we'd tried to build up had gone. Now Illy used to think a lot about this. He was a great thinker was Illy. He would never experiment when it wasn't necessary. I've heard folks call Illy selfish but that's rubbish. He batted and bowled for his side, or at least he did when I played with him.'

I suggested that Ray had been accused of meanness. Did Doug agree? The answer was predictably warm and spontaneous. 'Mean? Illy was always fair. He's nobody's fool and if that's being mean then he was mean. Was Arthur Mitchell mean because he wouldn't waste his time on someone who wasn't going to make it? But you could learn from him if you'd listen and be prepared to take a few bollockings.' I remembered Arthur saying to me not long before he died that when he appeared to be treating a young player harshly he was testing his character and trying to discover whether he could take criticism. He went on to say that when he first saw Doug and Ray in their early teens he had thought that if they didn't make the grade it was he that should get the sack. Mitchell was a perfectionist and it is no coincidence that Ray Illingworth, who respected and admired him, should share the same approach. I congratulated Illy a couple of years ago on a knock of seventy that had helped Leicestershire to their championship triumph and added that I'd heard he'd had an anxious start to the innings. He was incensed and claimed passionately that he'd played and missed twice in the first couple of overs and thereafter only once in the whole knock.

This is the brain of a cricketing computer, able to register and store for future use his own faults and errors as well as those of his opponents. (He was a great thinker was Illy!')

The dry, deadpan, almost pawky humour characteristic of some Yorkshiremen is very apparent when you talk to Doug Padgett. An example is the story of him and Ray batting together at Lord's in the days when batsmen were not allowed to appeal against the light. Both were desperately keen to get off out of the murk, and a ball from Alan Moss which pitched on the leg stump and went over the top of the off drew from Padgett at the non-striking end the comment, 'By, Mossy! That would have been a good one in daylight.' Sure enough next over they were off!

Doug and Ray travelled and roomed together for much of their careers with Yorkshire, and some of the former's recollections are penetrating and revealing. 'I used to moan a bit about the driving. Ray used to think he'd done all the bloody driving. I used to play on him a bit if it was his car. We'd 'appen done about fifty miles and I used to say, "I'm bloody tired, Illy," and he'd say, "You're all right, you've only just got going," and then I'd pretend to drop off and swerve a bit and pretend to wake up and he'd be driving in no time.' Illy later explained the justification of his nervousness. 'Let's face it, Padge could sleep on a clothes line, we've many a time taken him out of bed when we came back from breakfast and put him on the floor and he's still not woken up!'

Doug was not sure even now if his simple expedient was known to his travelling companion or not. 'I could see Illy used to wonder, 'I'm not right sure if he's kidding or not but if he isn't I'd better be driving for it's my bloody car." I remember when we were leaving a ground at six o'clock, he used to say, "Come on, bloody drive. I've just bowled thirty overs," and I used to say, "Aye, and I've just fetched the buggers back."

'He always used to pour our tea out in the morning 'cos I didn't go down for breakfast and invariably I'd drop off again and not drink it; then he'd come back up and wake me up and play bloody hell if I hadn't drunk this tea. "I'm not pouring your bloody tea out if you can't be bothered to sup it," so I used to have a little sip and pour the rest down the sink.' It was not just a question of thrift. The labourer was worthy of his hire in the form of a little appreciation, even if the labour were only the pouring of early morning tea.'

Frederick Sewards Trueman will be known to most readers as a purveyor of homely Yorkshire fun on television, as a face on a hoarding or, more probably to a reader of a cricket book, as a truly great fast bowler, whose status, wealth and worldwide renown have been squarely built upon his extraordinary hostility, physique, stamina and skill as one of the game's immortals. He is also in his own right a genuine wit, but one does not see or hear the best of Fred in pubs or clubs. Recently he was asked by some television interviewer what he would have done with the vandals who desecrated the Headingley wicket during the 1975 Australian Test and his reply was, 'I'd have chucked them off the pavilion onto t'tarmac, but I'm not a cruel man. I'd have given them a fifty-fifty chance. I'd have had Keith Fletcher underneath to catch them.'

Fred has become a legend in his own time, and having known him since his first first-class match, Cambridge University against Yorkshire at Fenner's in 1949, I have found him consistently friendly and helpful. He was more than ready to give his assessment of a colleague with whom he played for seventeen years and, predictably in the context of two human beings so diametrically opposed in attitude and temperament, admiration and respect were mixed with some reservations, the former predominating.

'If Raymond had played with any other county he'd have gone in number three or four and got two thousand runs easy. Playing with Yorkshire in the late 1950s and 1960s (and I'm sure we'll go down in history as a great side) many a time he had to throw his wicket away. To give him credit, he was never loth to do it for his side.

'I know a lot of folks wouldn't agree but I think that Raymond lacked self-confidence. You see the only thing I had against him in his cricketing was that he either didn't like to or wouldn't bowl on a good wicket and he wanted everything in his favour. He had an astute cricket brain and he was a far better all-rounder cricketer than the likes of David Allen and Fred Titmus. He spun the ball far more than Titmus and he'd got all the ability in the world.'

Fred recalled the wonderful affinity and happiness that had marked the Yorkshire side of the 1960s as not only a successful but a loyal and close-knit unit. What about the rows? 'Oh, we 'ad 'em. 'Ad to 'ave 'em. If I didn't agree with something Closey was doing I'd tell 'im and the sam wi' Raymond. I'd bloody tell 'im and he'd tell me. Raymond was very average-conscious and that's bad. He was always moaning about something but I sit and laugh when I hear some England cricketers talking about Raymond, especially his captaincy. When he wakes up in the morning he'll have forgotten more about cricket than they ever learned.' (Perhaps Fred has himself forgotten the occasion at Park Avenue when his luck was vile and the edged boundaries frequent. His reaction was a frustrated, 'These buggers are nicking me out of the averages!')

Like Arthur Mailey, Fred bowled like a millionaire, and Ray's mean, hard approach that would never willingly squander a single run inevitably resulted from a different attitude to life. Their route to the top in cricket had been very different. Fred burst upon the international scene with his spectacular successes against the Indians in 1952 so that he was a celebrity in his early twenties, while Ray tip-toed his way into Test cricket in 1958 with occasional matches, in which he rarely did himself justice, until he was appointed captain in 1969. A couple more of FST's memories must suffice to capture the shrewd, calculating side of Ray's make-up and the gloomy, almost calvinistic, belief that whoever else might be the recipient of good fortune it certainly would not be Illy himself.

'I remember in Philip Sharpe's great year, 1962, we were watching him at Taunton and Sharpey kept going "bang", through the covers for fower and Ray kept on moaning, "He's getting all the bad balls. They don't bowl bad 'uns to me!" Another time we were all talking about getting a rise (come to think of it, we were always on about getting a rise), and Raymond turns up one morning with a shopping list of how much everything cost — how much for potatoes and how much for bread and how much for electricity. He'd got it all worked out to a ha'penny. Some people are made like that but I couldn't live that way. Raymond has got a basic insecurity and it's not the home. I reckon that Raymond came from a twenty times better home than I did.

'Another time Roy Marshall was giving him the most fearful stick in a match at Scarborough at the end of the season,

Champion County v Runners-up it were, and Ray kept saying to Closey, "Get Fred on. I'm top of the averages", so I said to Closey, "Bloody keep 'im on. I'm not rushing up. I've been bowling all season." ' (A quick glance at *Wisden* confirms Fred's near-infallible memory. Illy's fears were not groundless as he finished third in the bowling averages to Jack Flavell and Brian Boshier!)

The criticisms Fred made of his old friend and colleague, namely that he tended to look after number one and that he was a moaner, must not hide his equally real respect and admiration; Ray, like Fred, is a 'plain blunt man' that 'speaks right on'. Doubtless there were times in the Yorkshire dressing-room and on the field when Fred Trueman was not the easiest or most diplomatic of people, but I'm sure he was sincere when he said, 'I'd like to think that as long as we're alive Raymond and I will be close and personal friends like we were when we were kids in 1948 and that in another forty years that we'll be sat talking together about the great days we've enjoyed. I'm delighted that Raymond has done so well in the last six years and I'm only sorry he hasn't done it for Yorkshire.'

After a particular Roses match at Leeds that Yorkshire's wicket-keeper would like to forget, Geoff Pullar, batting on a marled wicket on which the ball turned appreciably from the outset, was twice dropped behind the wicket off Illy and then survived a none too difficult stumping chance off the same bowler. The wicket-keeper was Jimmie Binks and in the bar afterwards he was standing sadly ruminating on the day's disasters, when an acquaintance of Ray came up to him and said passionately 'Hey, up, Raymond. We'd 'ave bowled 'em out if it 'adn't been for that silly bugger Binks.' Ray replied, 'Aye, we would. Meet Jimmie Binks.'

He's well worth the meeting. Just into his fifth decade, Jim is as dimpled and baby-faced as when he walked out onto the Trent Bridge turf for the first time as Yorkshire's wicket-keeper at the tender age of nineteen in June 1955. Roy Booth, who with Vic Wilson was the only Yorkshireman not to miss a Championship match in 1954, had been selected to keep wicket for the first half

40

of the season as characteristic Yorkshire thoroughness demanded that both he and Jimmie be given extended trials so that their relative merits could be accurately assessed and the right one retained to assume the mantle discarded by Don Brennan. The old principle of leaving a player in no doubt that there were others ready and able to take his place prompted Jimmie regularly to turn out for the county when he was on the walking wounded list.

Jimmie, who is employed by the J. H. Fenner Engineering firm in Hull, is shrewd and, like Fred, thoroughly articulate. Like most of his contemporaries, he was far from happy with the régime and atmosphere that obtained in those days. 'Even when we'd played for so many years it was as if the committee were trying to make you feel insecure; and this was in the sixties, when the side virtually picked itself — that is, often ten internationals and Tony Nicholson, who probably would have been one if it hadn't been for injury. The thing about Raymond was that it was in our interests for him not to be over-bowled. His biggest attribute was to bowl sides out when it was turning and I don't think he'd have done that so well if he'd had to graft away as a stock bowler. He was so good in the one-day game. In a three-day match he was rarely clobbered but if he was, it was always, "Get me off, skipper. I can't bowl at this bugger." I don't think he really wanted to leave Yorkshire when he did but I remember him saying, "I've had enough. Stuff 'em. I'm off. At least it might do you lads some good." ' Whether or not it did is open to question; however, like Padgett and Trueman, the respect with which Binks regarded Ray was not in doubt.

The only significant reservation that Jimmie Binks made was that Illy could be negative and defensive and that this tendency might be cited as sufficient cause to exclude him from the very highest echelons of captaincy to which the likes of Brian Sellers, Walter Robins and Richie Benaud belong.

7 *Money Matters*

When Illy was an established Farsley first-teamer the idea was rife among the uninitiated that amateur boots were filled with fivers; but travelling for away games was paid by the club and the only expenses that he drew, indeed the only remuneration of any sort that he received from the club, during one season in his late teens was 13s 10½d for travel to and from the club for home matches. He suggested tentatively that he should be allowed to play as a professional but this idea was not well received by the club. As pennies were scarce at home and remuneration during the time he worked for his father negligible, he gained an early appreciation of the lubricant effect a degree of prosperity exercises upon life's problems.

Since the inter-war years the path from professional cricket either to pub, club, the first-class umpire's list or public school has been well trodden, but in about the late 1940s and early 1950s a number of cricketers (among them Keith Miller, Sydney Barnes and Denis Compton) decided that fame was marketable; their activities heralded a new age of ghosted books, lucrative advertising, syndicated articles and 'image-creation' organised by highly-efficient but often uncompromising agents with no thought for or love of the game that had advanced the individual in question to the point at which he might be regarded as potential big business. Many might agree that the game of cricket has never been quite the same since.

All was well with county cricketers while many of their friends might be bringing home a weekly wage packet of two, three or four pounds before the war. Capped players with Yorkshire could make six or seven hundred pounds a year, which in those days was 'riches enough'. After the war wages in mine, shop, firm and factory spiralled astonishingly and soon it represented a real financial sacrifice for many cricketers to continue in the game. During the years when a young man would be striving for

43

acceptance and status in a firm or profession, the cricketer, often without certainty of eventual recognition or security, would be serving apprenticeship in one of the most exacting games, knowing full well he must become a household name nationally or at least locally before most firms would want to employ him.

If success came early, as it did to Fred Trueman, the decision was easier. Any fortune-making that Fred may have achieved has been at the game's periphery and after he had made a massive name for himself. In fact the largest sum, including Test matches, that he made out of cricket in any one year (excluding his benefit) was £1,601. Fred's recollections of his own experiences in this sphere are notable. 'If I was picked to play for England, I lost my Yorkshire match money. When I first played we got £75 a Test and tax had to come out of that. Now if I'd played for Yorkshire in a couple of away matches that would have been £44, plus win bonus probably, less expenses. I'd have brought back around £35. I've lost that and in the end I'm probably bowling my arse off for England for around fifteen quid.' No wonder that at both county and Test match level the independently-minded were required to fight every inch of the way to maintain or improve their lot.

One of the principal vocational hazards of the professional cricketer is to find an employer who requires his services for seven months of the year and will tolerate the news that he has been selected for a winter tour. This and other problems have directed cricketers at times into strange and varied occupations. (Harry Pilling of Lancashire has at various times found employment lugging bricks in a brickyard, carrying coal, driving a wagon, sticking handles onto umbrellas, working in a paper mill, for the Gas Board, as an apprentice butcher, as an apprentice tool-maker and as a representative for a coffin firm!)

Illy's National Service was followed by a further short period with his father and a spell coaching in South Africa in 1955; during the next winter he helped with the green-keeping at Fulneck Golf Club. Until 1959 he was concerned with a business venture in conjunction with his old Farsley Cricket Club friend Jimmie Claughton, selling sports goods, and when this folded the consequent vacuum was filled by the 1959-60 tour of

44

the West Indies. The next winter he virtually took as holiday, before touring Australia in 1962.

Now the name of Illingworth was known internationally, and when a local mill-owner offered Ray winter employment he may well have felt that the acquisition of a big name on the pay roll would be good for the firm's image. Illy tolerated this job for a couple of winters but learnt nothing, was poorly paid and without prospects; so, realising that he was wasting his time, he resigned and in 1963 joined the firm for which he still works, the Shaun Wilson Manufacturing Company, which sells fireworks and cards in the Huddersfield, Halifax, Sheffield and Bradford areas as well as in the Lowlands of Scotland. When expenses have been deducted from his remuneration it is clear he would not come near to managing if this were his only source of income, but since he can work out his own itinerary and diary of commitments he weaves this activity into a number of other projects. Illy has an interest in several business ventures, broadcasts regularly, appears on television and is in increasing demand as a cricket writer.

It is easy to see that the financial breakthrough came after he left Yorkshire at the end of the 1968 season in which he earned only £712. Even if he had played all the matches he could, including win money and match money, have earned no more than £1,500. Bear these figures in mind and recall the glamour and adulation and the very real (to him shattering) contrast with the monetary reward of Illy's brother professionals in football and golf, and it is not surprising that a canny and calculating person like Ray Illingworth should have experienced a developing awareness of the importance and value of money.

Those who have money find it easy to be blandly casual on the subject. (A friend with semi-aristocratic, public school background said to me recently, 'Of all the subjects I find really boring, money is outstandingly the most boring of all.') To appreciate the value of money it is essential to have experienced a time when you were poor. It was not so bad when Ray was a young bachelor, but marriage accentuated the magnitude of the problem.

In his services days, he used to beg a trip into Leeds on the night-school bus from Dishforth, profiting from the opportunity of studying human psychology and the technique of film by taking Shirley, eventually to become his wife, to the pictures!

They were married in 1958. Ray had saved about £1,500. Shirley had £500, left to her by her grandfather, and her parents lent the young couple another £500, so they commenced their married life with £2,500 at their disposal. They bought their house for £2,100, spent between £300 and £400 on furnishing two rooms and found that they then scarcely possessed a penny between them. Shirley worked for three years before the birth of their first daughter, Vicki, and having paid back the money owing to her parents they started to save again. Clearly, if Shirley had not gone out to work, the Illingworths at this stage, earning in the region of £1,200 from Yorkshire and with winter employment a real problem, would have found themselves close to the breadline; as in others this has left a legacy of bitterness.

The feeling was one of frustration. Yorkshire, the premier county from 1959 to Ray's departure, won seven championships out of ten but were more poorly paid than many cricketers from other counties. Unlike his present county, Yorkshire in those days made little attempt to help players with winter employment, and the suspicion, whether or not it was justified, was that the authorities were quite happy to see a player entirely dependent upon the remuneration he received from the county.

During the 1960s, when it was clearly possible for the Yorkshire cricketers to negotiate from a position of strength, Illy was as meticulous in his examination of his and his colleagues' rights and wrongs as he was in his wholehearted performance on the field. He has been misquoted and misunderstood in this context; an example can be cited from the now famous (or notorious) Extraordinary General Meeting of the Yorkshire County Cricket Club in 1970, during which Brian Sellers accused him of asking for more money than the rest of the Yorkshire players. As Ray was in Australia at the time, he was unable to answer this allegation. The point seems to be so basic and crucial that he must be allowed to speak for himself. 'I never argued for more money for myself. I believed we should all get the same. Of the three senior players, Brian Close, Fred

Trueman and myself, I was the only one who said we should be paid the same. I could see their argument but the way I looked at it was over a period of, say, ten years. When I first got my cap I certainly wasn't worth what Len got but when I became a senior player and Don Wilson arrived, he wasn't worth what I got but over the period it had evened itself out. I said we should all be better paid and then there'd be no quibbles and niggles and we'd gain more by all playing for each other.'

Illy is good at many things but he is not good at forgiving what he regards as a wrong or a slight. He has been accused of having a chip on his shoulder. If the charge is justified, it must be judged in conjunction with an equally well-developed sense of gratitude to and appreciation of those whom he believes have helped him and can genuinely be regarded as friends.

The vast majority of human beings are infinitely more the product of background, influence and experience than of the amalgam of qualities and characteristics with which the roulette wheel of heredity has provided them. Illy is no exception. Since his establishment in the Yorkshire side, he had been under constant tension. Consider the pressures outlined in previous chapters and add to them the very real financial problems that marriage brought in 1958 and it is easy to realise just how near Ray was to becoming a permanently disaffected barrack-room lawyer, a shop steward whom no sane committee would have invited to captain Ossett NALGO, let alone Leicestershire or England. That he did not was largely because of two developments, the one logically sired by the other: the advent of Ronnie Burnet and the era of success for Yorkshire which his short term as captain initiated, comparable with the triumphs of the 1920s and 1930s.

8 *Sanity*

Ronnie Burnet first heard of his appointment to captain Yorkshire when he read it in an evening paper, prior to the 1958 season. He had been entrusted with an explosive situation at a crucial stage in the county's history; certainly there was something symbolic in the manner in which he received the information. Following Norman Yardley's retirement in 1955, Billy Sutcliffe, a pleasant person and a fine batsman, always dogged by the spectre of his distinguished father, had skippered the side for two years. In the words of *Wisden*, 'During the two years Sutcliffe held the position he tried his utmost to infuse new life into the team but it must be said that he did not always receive the support his efforts deserved.'

Burnet must have been aware that he had been appointed to fire bullets. Willie Watson, perhaps Yorkshire's finest batsman since Hutton's retirement, had left to join Leicestershire at the end of the 1957 season and Ronnie Burnet learnt in mid-season again from an evening paper, that the Yorkshire committee had decided to dispense with the services of Frank Lowson and Bob Appleyard at the end of the season. He had not been consulted and, as a friendly and fair-minded man, was sufficiently incensed to reply to the casual greeting of Clifford Hesketh, then chairman of cricket, 'No, everything's not all right. I was not consulted but if I had been I'd have asked you to sack three not two! And the third would have been Johnny Wardle.'

It is unfortunate that such a wonderful cricketer has to be portrayed critically, and there is another side to him that is far more estimable. While over-keenness could account for many of Bob Appleyard's oddities and misdemeanours, there is no doubt that Wardle was sometimes bloody-minded for the sake of bloody-mindedness and consequently a disruptive influence. Two incidents decided Burnet that reformation or departure was the only answer. Playing against Derbyshire at Chesterfield on a really sticky wicket, Wardle was virtually unplayable. Bowling flat and slightly short, he was turning too much to hit the edge of the bat, so that Arnold Hamer and Charlie Lee (two Yorkshire expatriates) managed to survive when they should not have done so. Ron suggested to Johnny Wardle that he should bowl a fuller length so that the ball would turn less and received a real mouthful, liberally larded with procreative imagery and epithets. 'I've been bowling for fifteen years and you come into the side your first season in the game and tell me how to bowl. Piss off!' Burnet waited a couple of overs and then told Wardle he would like him to relieve Illingworth at the other end where he thought the ball would not turn so much. After informing his captain that 'he must be out of his bloody mind', Wardle proceeded to go on at the other end and bowl six deliveries around the length Trueman would have employed to bowl a bouncer, five of which were hit for four by one of the Derbyshire batsmen. The sixth required a titanic dive and stop by Doug Padgett to prevent another boundary.

The other event concerned yet another dropped catch off Wardle's bowling. As in the Cowan incident, the culprit had apologised and as Johnny had patted him on the shoulder, apparently suggesting sympathy and tolerance, he had muttered something sufficiently vituperative to contrast strongly with the visual impression received by the crowd.

The truth was that time and again appearance differed from reality. Johnny Wardle could be superbly funny, without apparently possessing the warmth of character that enjoyed the happiness uncomplicated laughter can create. Once he had the crowd in paroxysms of laughter, having hidden a player's bat under the umpire's coat while he attended to bootlace or pad, and, as the appreciative mirth reached a climax, he said, 'Just listen to the silly bastards.'

After the news of Wardle's dismissal had become public knowledge, the current match, against Somerset at Bramall Lane, became something closely resembling hell for Burnet. He was booed to the echo as resoundingly as Wardle was cheered and his reaction was understandably a dejected feeling of bewilderment that, unpaid and indeed losing money for the privilege of captaining Yorkshire, he should be subjected to this sort of treatment; but popular hatred soon turned to sympathetic approval, equally loudly voiced, when Wardle burst into print in a series of articles that effectively ended his first-class career, the first being based on the theme that Yorkshire were carrying their captain. It was a tragic, premature close to the career of a great bowler. Only six Yorkshiremen have taken more wickets for the county.

The 1958 season was perilously close to being a disastrous one for Yorkshire, though Illy, demonstrating encouraging form with bat and ball, reacted as he did throughout his career to leadership he found respectable and firm yet fair. An even more pertinent tribute to Burnet's methods was to be found in Doug Padgett, of whom he had made an issue when accepting the captaincy. He was told, 'Certainly give Padgett his cap, if you must but you'll find he's off in a year or two. He's just not good enough.' (Not good enough! The following year, Padgett and Illingworth, the two most highly-placed Yorkshiremen in the first-class averages, scored 2,181 and 1,726 runs respectively, and the latter completed a wonderful season that helped Yorkshire to their unpredictable championship success with 110 wickets, putting him second in both county batting and bowling averages.)

But the cracks were only thinly papered over and it needed another season for the decor to show to advantage. Treatment had been drastic but the patient recovered with an abruptness that startled even the surgeons. Brian Sellers, who succeeded Clifford Hesketh as chairman in 1959, thought that the rebuilding process would probably need about three years before Yorkshire could hope to challenge for another championship; the heady triumph of 1959 restored faith in human nature. Team spirit was not a pretentious myth. Above all the cricketing truth was confirmed that, though a captain may not appear on paper to be worth his place, his independence of mind, skilful man-management and dedication to the side can in aggregate prove to be invaluable.

Since his services days, Ray had rarely played his cricket in a happy atmosphere. Suddenly the scene was transformed. One must not over-sentimentalise but, knowing and liking Ronnie

51

Burnet, I find it hard not to do so. He is so essentially a kindly man. Cheerful, loyal and uncomplicated he is the sort of person who inspires confidence, with whom one would wish to share a problem or a crisis, and above all he is a man blessed with the priceless gift of taking pleasure from the successes of others. Mischief (which I hope will not offend) prompts me to add that he is not therefore a typical Yorkshire county cricketer! It is no exaggeration to suggest that with the short reign of Ronnie Burnet Ray Illingworth began to swing back onto an even keel. He might still bemoan his ill luck. He might try to avoid the lengthy stint of bowling on the perfect wicket, and he certainly did not overnight turn into a cross between Albert Schweitzer and Dr Barnardo, but the danger of his corruption had passed. Sanity had been restored.

The 1959 season opened auspiciously for Yorkshire's captain. Coming in to bat against Nottinghamshire at Acklam Park, Middlesborough, not always the easiest wicket on which to survive let alone dominate, Ronnie Burnet cannot have been enraptured with a total of 99 for 5, but his stand of 61 with his ultimate successor as captain, Vic Wilson, swung the game Yorkshire's way and his own 47 was the second highest score in Yorkshire's first innings. Trueman and Ryan hustled Notts out in their first innings and Don Wilson and Illingworth in their second, though it needed spectacular enterprise from Bryan Stott and Ken Taylor, whose century occupied only 115 minutes, to engineer a situation from which Burnet could confidently declare.

Victory by 194 runs in this first crucial match was worth more than the actual points that accrued. A positive, attacking note had been struck, which was to re-echo throughout a season that saw Yorkshire plummet to the depths before clawing their way back in one of the most truly remarkable performances in the history of the County Championship.

Nothing, we have always been told, succeeds like success, an aphorism that Ronnie Burnet's young side proceeded to demonstrate. Suddenly cricket was fun again and the new spirit in the side was illustrated by the excesses of enthusiasm of that super-enthusiast, Don Wilson. Well may Fred Trueman (perhaps with the bad old days in mind) claim that with himself and ten Don Wilsons he could 'win t'championship for you on keenness alone'. In a sense this was what actually occurred. Never did Don's fanatical belief that every ball he bowled was the unplayable delivery, the blueprint for which was hidden away in some cricketing Valhalla, waver for a moment. Up would go the arms and around would go the body in a crazy, writhing ballet of uninhibited optimism, even if the ball, like most of its predecessors, had been confidently met by the middle of the bat. As a fielder, Don was superb. He made short mid-wicket assume the status and significance of cover-point on the legside, from which position he must have engineered more run-outs than almost any other cricketer of modern times. Pounded and battered, his near-infallible left hand became in his latter years vulnerable to injury as the webbing between thumb and forefinger split progressively more readily; but despite the fact that Don's histrionic antics guaranteed him his fair share of mockery, he was an under-rated bowler whose prodigalities of flight naturally complemented Illy's scientific precision. When the ball turned, Ray would probably win Yorkshire the match, whereas on a plumb 'un his nagging accuracy at one end would often encourage fatal indiscretion off Wilson's tantalising parabola. In 1959 Don was very much in the apprentice stage, but they were to develop into an effective combination.

There were few signs initially that the championship was to return to its rightful home. After six weeks the county still languished half way up the table owing to a patchy collective performance that had not inspired undue optimism in the Ridings, before three successive wins thrust them into first place. Sussex, Warwickshire and Essex were the victims and Ray got runs or wickets or both in all three games. Another crucial win earlier in the season must have recalled vivid memories of his baptism at Headingley eight years earlier. This time it was Derek Shackleton, who with Vic Cannings, Yorkshire's tormentor on the earlier occasion, bowled Yorkshire to 44 for 4 at Hull, when Ray joined Bryan Stott; they added eighty-six priceless runs that wrenched the initiative back from Hampshire, with Stott's fine batting in each innings translating probable

53

defeat into exhilarating victory.

So much for the good news. What of the bad? A combination of those time-honoured aliases, Smith and Brown of Gloucestershire, gobbled up Yorkshire for thirty-five runs at Bristol, in August, in hazy overcast conditions that allowed the ball to swing like a cut serve; this was the lowest total for which the county had been dismissed in twenty-four years. Gloucestershire won by an innings and seventy-seven runs, though their own very real Championship hopes disintegrated in the following match when they were beaten by the reigning champions, Surrey. The narrowness of Yorkshire's defeat, by sixteen runs to Somerset at Bath, in the match immediately preceding can have represented scant consolation. Were Surrey to add an eighth triumph to their seven successive championships?

It would have been doubly frustrating to Yorkshire eyes if this had been the case. Both Ray Illingworth, so often the steely reinforcement to Yorkshire's middle order batting as well as their front-line spinner, and the explosive Fred Trueman were helping England to their innings victory over India at the Oval; but they were back for the next match at Worcester, claiming over half the Worcester wickets between them in addition to forty not out from Ray, when the crucial stage-setting match was won and Yorkshire travelled south-east, knowing that victory at Hove would mean that Surrey's fingers had been prised from the championship at last.

9 The Great Match

Before we recall the stirring events against Sussex at Hove a glance at a couple of the many other matches that helped Yorkshire to her Championship confirm the qualities and developing authority that were fashioning Illy into the cricketer he was still to become. *Wisden* recalls in the general comment on Yorkshire's 1959 season that they 'could scarcely be called lucky for no fewer than twenty times did Burnet lose the toss and the county batted first in only six matches'. Surely here the 'good book' is nodding. The fact that Burnet's young and enthusiastic Yorkshire side were so effective chasing a total in the fourth innings accounted for their success more than any other single factor, apart from outstandingly good team spirit. Yorkshire never considered any target too daunting to be wholeheartedly assailed, and in the Worcester match just mentioned a draw seemed certain at lunch on the last day; but the last seven Worcester wickets fell for twenty-seven runs and again Yorkshire won against the clock after a mad scamper.

Against Essex at Colchester at the end of June, Illy provided further confirmation of the fighting qualities he contributed to the middle order of the Yorkshire and, later, England batting. Having bowled Essex out for 189, Yorkshire slid to 62 for 4 with the match still balanced when Ray came in; when he was last out the total was 329 and his own share a superb 150. A fierce assault on the middle order and tail by Fred Trueman at his most hostile counteracted their sound start, and after Essex were all out Yorkshire were left with 86 to win in 45 minutes.

It was still the era of separate dressing rooms for amateurs and professionals, so that Ronnie Burnet was lodging with those two forthright and articulate individuals, Doug Insole and Trevor Bailey; Ron recalls that in the interval prior to the match's last innings Trevor Bailey remarked that with the correct fields placed for himself and Barry Knight it would be totally impossible for Yorkshire to get the runs and proceeded to facilitate the task of his captain by drawing a plan of the two relevant sets of field placings on a piece of paper. Burnet's answer was to un-leash the unpredictable and explosive Trueman at the fall of the first wicket. Fred's thirty-three not out, scythed, mown and battered, combined with useful supporting knocks from Bryan Stott and Brian Close to see Yorkshire safely home. This, of course, was an example of inspired improvisation triumphing over cerebral professionalism, as consistently practised and advocated by Ray as much as by Trevor Bailey. A glance at the Essex second innings bowling figures reveals the intensity of the onslaught. Bailey's read: 4.5 — 0 — 40 — 3, and Knight's were 4 — 0 — 44 — 0. For a lively, seam and swing bowler of Barry Knight's capabilities to concede eleven an over and his dis-tinguished partner almost as many nudges the match firmly into the realms of the bizarre.

The other match deserving particular scrutiny was played at Headingley on 8, 10 and 11 August against Kent, and hindsight confers upon it considerable significance. The Saturday, during which Kent batted, was steaming hot and the awesomely poor form of David Pickles meant that Yorkshire, with Fred absent, were in effect two bowlers short, in the face of sound batting from Arthur Phebey and Colin Cowdrey at his most command-ing. In this context Ray Illingworth and Don Wilson bore most of the burden of the afternoon's toil. Illy had taken none for 46 in 24 overs and Don a creditable 5 for 67 off 29.2 overs, when the innings ended after close on an hour's play on the Monday, during which just seven more runs were added.

When it had transpired during an after-play drink on Saturday night that Colin Cowdrey was not declaring on Monday morn-ing, as was the normal convention in county cricket then, Ronnie Burnet had asked him, 'As a matter of interest, why not?' Cowdrey said it was because of the negative, defensive tactics employed by Yorkshire in the person of Don Wilson, who, he alleged, holding up thumb and forefinger to make around a three inch span, 'had been bowling consistently this much wide of the off stump'!

Now another significant development had occurred during the

closing stages on the Saturday. Brian Close had bowled a good stint in the match but when asked to come on by his captain during the last session had broken down and announced that he was completely unable to bowl owing to a bruised heel. It was not the first time that this sort of thing had happened, so Burnet, realising the need for drastic measures, demanded and received a full medical report, which made it clear that in the examiner's opinion there was no medical reason why he should not be able to bowl. Close, moreover, played two rounds of golf on the Sunday.

At the battle front things were far from comfortable for Yorkshire, who, caught in heavy conditions, were struggling on the Monday, especially in the persons of Stott, Taylor and Padgett, to avoid a debacle. Wickets fell, with no easing of the conditions, and, declaring 134 behind, Burnet hoped that Cowdrey would invite Yorkshire to one of the last innings chases to which they had become so accustomed. That they got the chance to perform one was entirely because of the astonishing return of 8 for 41 from Brian Close (who had been too crippled to bowl at all on Saturday evening!); moreover, he achieved these figures largely bowling out-swingers at brisk and hostile medium pace! This remarkable achievement left Yorkshire needing 244 to win in two hours and fifty-five minutes. *Wisden* states that 'Yorkshire won with two minutes to spare.' Ronnie Burnet's memory of the match, so pertinent and penetrating in the light of Illy's confidence and character, is a little different; 'We still needed eight to win off what would have definitely been the last over and Raymond was sixty-something not out. He went up to Bob Platt (I think it was) and said to him, 'Whether you hit it or not, run.'' Alan Brown was bowling. Bob missed it and Ray got home, leaving him five balls to win the match. He pulled the first two for four and there we were at the top of the table with Surrey pushed into second place. What impressed me so much was the way that Raymond took charge at the end. It was nothing whatever to do with captaincy. I was in the pavilion. It was Raymond, not thinking about what might go wrong but taking on himself the full responsibility for the situation.'

How warmly one echoes Burnet's sentiments. There are

cricketers who would prefer to walk off after a drawn game with 66 not out to their name, rather than risk being out going for a win. There are also those who might have lacked the initiative to instruct the batsman at the striking end to run whether or not he hit the ball. The qualities of the high-class captain, doubtless latent in Illy, were beginning to emerge and become apparent.

The title of this chapter is intentionally misleading. It was not a 'great' match but a great ninety-eight minutes following a rather dull, disappointing and sometimes acrimonious contest. Two ingredients were crucial to the Yorkshire camp in the first three innings that preceded the last wild, incredible scamper, one positive, the other negative. Fred Trueman, shattered with fatigue after a prodigiously tough season, could not drive himself to marshal the pace needed to embarrass Sussex or, more to the point, did not himself believe that he could do so. On the credit side, Ray Illingworth again held his finger in the split dyke of the middle order with help from fellow-spinners Jack Birkenshaw and Don Wilson. Illy came in to bat with Yorkshire having slipped to 38 for 3 and without his truly sterling knock of 122 there would have been no lead of 97 and no chance of the sort of platform, however rickety, from which the final attack could have been launched.

Sussex gave real trouble, well though Ray and Don Wilson bowled. Everybody seemed to get runs and by lunch on the last day a declaration, had it been forthcoming, would have set Yorkshire a target in the region of a hundred runs per hour; but Robin Marlar made it quite clear that under no circumstances would he consider declaring. After all, Yorkshire was Yorkshire and he did not wish to risk the suggestion that he had handed the old enemy their first championship since 1946 on a plate. Several of the Sussex players did not appear to share this view and one of the three wickets to fall in the forty minutes that Sussex batted after lunch, that of Ian Thomson, appeared to be sacrificed against orders.

When the Yorkshire side regained the decent privacy of their dressing room, the atmosphere resembled that of the Tory Central Office or Transport House following a lost election. The theme of Burnet's words to his side was simple enough: 'Well, lads. Do we go for it as we've done all year or do we admit that it's just not on?' Ronnie admits now that he and his side were 'pig sick' but after it was agreed that the 'impossible' should be undertaken universal joy was not apparent when he announced that Doug Padgett would bat only one place below his normal position of number three. Opinion was virtually universal that his best scoring rate would be grossly inadequate to the needs of the moment. At this stage even the presence of Harry Secombe in the Yorkshire dressing room was unable to counteract the general gloom.

Burnet dropped Brian Bolus down the order and opened with Taylor and Stott. The Sussex members sat up as far as deck chairs would allow when fifteen came from the first over, including a straight six struck by Stott off the first ball of the innings. Close succeeded Taylor who was leg before to Dexter and a couple of precious minutes were lost when Close hit one of the longest sixes of the season, miles it seemed over the scoreboard. When he was out for a modest twelve, Yorkshire had reached 40 for 2 in thirteen minutes and Robin Marlar had seven men on the boundary. Bryan Stott had been as piratical as ever and when Doug Padgett, the orthodox, classical stroke-maker, came to the wicket, Bryan was twenty-seven not out. Ronnie Burnet's instructions to Padgett had been to 'score off every ball', and the fact that the field was well and truly spread by his arrival must have facilitated this objective.

There are some wonderfully good runners-between-wickets in County Cricket today, among them Roger Tolchard, Frank Hayes and Clive Radley, but all to whom I have talked about the Hove match are agreed that Padgett and Stott were supreme. Sussex, disintegrating in the face of Stott's broadsword and Padgett's rapier, conceded a scoring rate that virtually settled the match and the destination of the championship. When Padgett was first out for a breath-taking seventy-nine, he had batted only just over an hour and had almost overtaken the forceful Stott. Yorkshire had reached a score of 181 for 3 after seventy-three minutes when Padgett, his normally rubicund countenance doubtless verging upon puce, was back in the pavilion; it was now a gentle stroll to victory, though Trueman and Stott, caught off Marlar four short of a truly memorable hundred, perished before Brian Bolus leg glanced the winning runs. For forty-five minutes it was impossible to move in the Yorkshire dressing-room. I'm certain that two voices must have rung out above the rest, those of F. Trueman and H. Secombe. What a duet they must have made!

This is an age of awards. Always, it seems, there has to be a 'Man of the Match' and sometimes the team suffers. As Ronnie Burnet stammered out his tribute to the wonderful spirit of his own side, he must have been grateful not to have had to award a 'Man of the Match' at Hove from the six candidates who presented themselves: Stott — 34 and 96; Padgett — 79 in the winning scamper; Illingworth — 122 and 5 not out in addition to match figures of 7 for 117; Taylor — 4 for 40 off 22 overs in the first innings; Birkenshaw — 38 in the first innings and four fine catches to help dismiss Sussex in their second knock; and of course Wilson — 55 in the first innings and four out of the first five Sussex batsmen in their second innings for 78 off 24 overs. My own guess is that if the decision had been left to the Yorkshire players they would have given the 'award' to Burnet himself, whose contribution to the season may have been inconsiderable statistically but in terms of real leadership, based upon encouragement, discipline and an unwavering resolve to treat each member of his team as an individual, could not be exaggerated.

The win at Hove was, of course, a victory for the real game of cricket as opposed to the myth of first-class cricket, based as it so often is upon the chess-like manoeuvrings of players and captains who are not prepared to act or to think independently of the other party. How often have we heard the dreary conversations about how a certain captain has 'bowled his seamers to a defensive field' or 'only bowled so many overs an hour while we bowled so many more' or 'killed the game stone dead by his declaration' or, most time-honoured and indefensible of the lot, 'how can I play shots? The ball isn't coming onto the bat.' (An intelligent and witty old gentleman some years ago had watched with rapture a sparkling attacking innings by Majid on a slow wicket for Glamorgan and was heard to mutter, 'The secretary should make a public apology on Majid's behalf. The poor

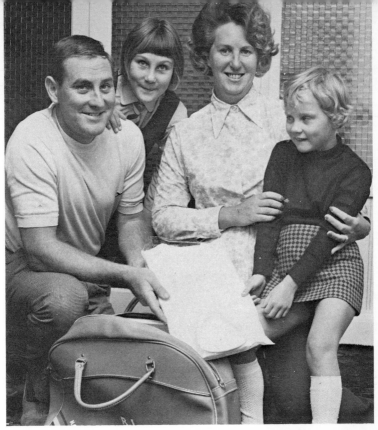

1 Shirley and the two girls, Vicki and Diane, help with preparations for the 1970-71 tour of Australia. *(Photograph: Bradford & District Newspaper Co. Ltd.)*

2 A kiss for the new Mrs. Illingworth from best man, Brian Close, at Illy's wedding, 1958. *(Photograph: Bradford & District Newspaper Co. Ltd.)*

3 Watched by the author's namesake behind the wickets for Hampshire, Illy hits out in Leicestershire's victorious Benson and Hedges Final in 1975. *(Photograph: Patrick Eagar)*

4 Straight from the coaching manual! Note the braced left leg and evidence of full pivot.
(Photograph: Patrick Eagar)

5 R. W. Morgan of New Zealand bowled by Illy's outswinger, Leeds 1965. The ball has hit the off stump with the batsman clearly intending to play to the on side. *(Photograph: Sport & General Press Agency)*

6 Illy introduces his team to the Queen during the Lord's Test against the West Indies in 1969. David Brown is shaking hands with Her Majesty. *(Photograph: Sport & General Press Agency)*

7 Illy and Colin Cowdrey find a singleness of purpose in fielding practice that was not so apparent on the 1970-71 tour of Australia. *(Photograph: Central Press Photos Ltd.)*

8 Illy gets one away on the leg side during his side's second innings in the second test match in Perth which ended in a draw. 1970 *(Photograph: Central Press Photos Ltd.)*

9 John Snow just warming up in Melbourne. 1971 *(Photograph: Central Press Photos Ltd.)*

10 Illy bowled by John Gleeson. Illy turns in time to see the stumps shattered. 1971 *(Photograph: Central Press Photos Ltd.)*

11 John Snow has an expression of grim determination on his face as he sends down a delivery whilst practising in Melbourne. 1971 *(Photograph: Central Press Photos Ltd.)*

12 John Snow grabbed by spectators after Terry Jenner was hit on the head by a bumper from Snow. 1971 *(Photograph: Central Press Photos Ltd.)*

13 Geoff Boycott run out in England's first innings of the sixth test match in Adelaide. 1971 *(Photograph: Central Press Photos Ltd.)*

14 Greg Chappell returns G. Boycott's bat after Boycott had thrown it to the ground and refused to walk to the pavilion. 1971 *(Photograph: Central Press Photos Ltd.)*

15 Geoff Boycott. 1971 *(Photograph: Central Press Photos Ltd.)*

16 Illy being caught out by Ian Redpath for 41. Bowler was Gleeson. Melbourne. 1971 *(Photograph: Central Press Photos Ltd.)*

17 Illy looks at Peter Lever's whitlowed finger. 1971 *(Photograph: Central Press Photos Ltd.)*

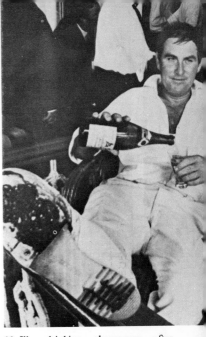

18 John Edrich and Brian Luckhurst chair captain Ray Illingworth off the Sydney cricket ground. 1971 (*Photograph: Central Press Photos Ltd.*)

19 Illy drinking champagne after winning The Ashes in Sydney. 1971 (*Photograph: Central Press Photos Ltd.*)

20 Illy knotting his Taverners tie shortly after being presented with it by the former 'Taverners' club president, Sir Robert Menzies, in Sydney. 1971 (*Photograph: Central Press Agency*)

21 Another victim for Derek Underwood during England's victory against Australia at Leeds in 1972 as Illy catches John Inverarity at silly point. *(Photograph: Patrick Eagar)*

22 Illy catches Paul Sheahan at the second attempt, again off Underwood in the same match, Leeds 1972. *(Photograph: Patrick Eagar)*

23 Illy's sweep. Gary Sobers takes evasive action. England v West Indies, Oval 1973. *(Photograph: Patrick Eagar)*

24 But close fielding has its dangers. Illy is injured at the Oval 1972, England v Australia. *(Photograph: Patrick Eagar)*

25 Mike Turner, the Leicestershire secretary, and Illy celebrate victory with their team in the John Player League, 1974. *(Photograph: Patrick Eagar)*

26 A second victory in the Benson and Hedges Cup Final, Lord's 1975. *(Photograph: Patrick Eagar)*

27 A second victory in the Benson and Hedges Cup Final, Lord's 1975. *(Photograph: Patrick Eagar)*

28 The Illingworth family at Buckingham Palace to receive Illy's CBE, 1973. *(Photograph Keystone Press Agency Ltd.)*

29 A study in technical perfection and concentration. This one will land on a length and a line. Look at the finger action. *(Photograph: Patrick Eager)*

fellow doesn't appear to know that the ball isn't coming onto the bat!')

A high-class captain or indeed cricketer will (and must, if the game is going to retain its potential dynamism) refuse to allow his tactical approach or performance to be unduly influenced by that of the opposition; given a fair chance of establishing ascendancy or indeed achieving eventual victory, he must not fall back upon the threadbare arguments listed above to hide his lack of enterprise and imagination but must take the situation as it is and attempt to 'remould it nearer to the heart's desire'.

When Ronnie Burnet finally left Hove, after a lengthy interview for the BBC, he drove via London to be interviewed by ITV and thence north by himself, as his normal travelling companion, Doug Padgett, had at his suggestion gone on with the rest of the team. Physically exhausted, he fell asleep at the wheel near Wakefield but managed to reach his home in Baildon to pick up clean clothes for Scarborough, though the last leg of the long journey was beyond him and he slept in an empty house, as his family had already left for the Festival.

Contrast this with the triumphant arrival of the rest of the Yorkshire side at the Balmoral Hotel in Scarborough in the small hours, where more champagne and a royal reception awaited them; but when Burnet and indeed each of the Yorkshire players arrived at the ground the following morning they were cheered every step to the pavilion in a welcome that none of them will forget as long as he lives.

Ray Illingworth, in unstoppable form with the bat, contributed 105 and 35, both not out, in an action re-play of Hove for the benefit of Yorkshire supporters at Scarborough; set 260 to win in two and a half hours, victory against MCC came on this occasion with twenty-five minutes to spare and by sixty-six runs in the Champion County versus The Rest at the Oval a week later, Ray scoring a couple of thirties and, in harness with Brian Close, spinning Yorkshire to victory after they had recovered from the ignominy of following on in the first innings. Further evidence of Yorkshire's fabulous team spirit could be found in the fact that the players clubbed together to pay for Harold Bird to make the trip to the Oval as he had not been selected. Jackie Birkenshaw was twelfth man and it was felt by the authorities that it would be an unwarranted extravagance to take an extra player down to London, but Bird was spared the disappointment of missing the season's last match through the generosity of his colleagues.

There was another significant development that spun off from the Champion County v The Rest. Vic Wilson, the senior professional, who had not commanded a regular place in the side during the season, was selected and helped to win the match with a fighting second innings century. Many thought it would be his last match for Yorkshire. When, with characteristic unselfishness, Burnet decided to resign, having done the job he had been appointed to do, namely to encourage and develop a new attitude and corporate morale in the side, it was Vic Wilson who was appointed to be his successor; it is sad to recall that the news of Burnet's resignation was sold for the sum of five pounds to a national newspaper by a member of the Yorkshire committee.

Burnet, drained at the end of the season to the point of complete mental and physical exhaustion, is to be envied for the happiness and satisfaction he had experienced and imparted. His short reign had a profound influence upon Ray Illingworth; the essential character and credo of the man who was to win back the Ashes for England and revitalise Leicestershire had been formed and would not be basically modified.

10 The Cricketer — Good Or Great?

In the 1960 *Wisden*'s 'Five Cricketers of the Year', Bill Bowes, his coach and a considerable influence on his bowling, writes of Ray Illingworth: 'the wonderful summer of 1959, with firm, true pitches, gave Illingworth the opportunity to blossom. He showed an ability to fashion an innings for the occasion. He could defend hard or hit hard. He lofted the ball with certainty high and wide of mid-on. He punched powerfully from the back foot to the covers. It was the same with his bowling. On helpful wickets he spun the ball. On good wickets he was miserly or prepared to buy at any price as the situation demanded.'

In attempting to assess the status of any cricketer it is impossible to ignore competition and opportunity. A wicket-keeper may be the second best in the country but if he belongs to the county with the best then he is bound to languish as deputy or depart. What is apparent in the words quoted above from a great cricketer and shrewd judge of the game is that Bowes is describing a complete cricketer, equipped to provide a tough, effective, professionally competent performance in all circumstances. This was apparent in his fielding. I have referred to the number of catches Illy took in the outfield off the bowling of Johnny Wardle, but it was as a gully fielder that he built a reputation for reliability and, at times, brilliance, and that particular position, especially when F. S. Trueman was in his prime, was not a post to be occupied by the faint-hearted. Even now, in his mid-forties, Ray is no slouch in the field and can offer a standard of competence that must cheer him to some degree in compensation for aching joints and periodic back trouble; in a recent match against Lancashire he caught the powerful Bernard Reidy from a perfectly struck on-drive at short mid-wicket off the bowling of Graham McKenzie with an unobtrusive ease and confidence that completely masked the genuine difficulty of the catch. Some young players who besport themselves with the larger ball during the winter months would have celebrated with a lap of honour or at least a quick hug!

Most Yorkshiremen detest superlatives. The story is told of the great Wilfred Rhodes, who, when called upon to give his assessment of a famous Test cricketer, feasted, fêted and admired throughout the length and breadth of the cricketing world, replied after due pause for consideration, 'Aye, 'e were useful.' It is a fact that there are three gradations of cricketing prowess, the boundaries of which are well-defined and instantly recognisable to the élite. Wilfred Rhodes may well have employed the epithet 'useful' in order to correct what he regarded as an unfortunate tendency towards over-enthusiastic adulation, but it is nevertheless the one used to describe the average run-of-the-mill county cricketer who does a good job for his side but cannot realistically hope for advancement close to or into the dizzy heights of Test cricket.

The next category is a 'good player', which suggests that a cricketer must be close to international honours, while the rare use of the word 'great' will place a player alongside the game's relatively few immortals. Vocabulary like coinage can easily become debased, and it is a sign of the times that too often in the written and spoken branches of the media every goal, every innings, every try and sometimes one feels every sportsman is described as 'great'.

Is Raymond Illingworth a 'great' cricketer? Before attempting an answer to this question one must try to place him, judged by the highest standards, in his appropriate category as batsman and bowler. Ever since the early 1950s it has been his bowling that has commanded primary attention; yet it should not be forgotten that if the correct definition of an all-rounder is a cricketer who would command selection for his ability either as a batsman or as a bowler then Illy is clearly one of the comparatively few current English players to whom this applies. One of the keys to an understanding of his success is the diligence with which he has gone on studying his craft and therefore improving. The soft-shoe shuffle to the wicket, the lowish arm at delivery (perhaps to achieve more purchase), the classic sideways-on position and the braced left leg, reminiscent of a class golfer's position at impact, may not appear to have changed much over the years, but unlike most cricketers he has somehow managed to become an appreciably better bowler after his mid-thirties than he was before: or has he? Perhaps his considerable skills have remained the same and the overall standard of his opponents both at Test and county level are nothing like as good as they were in the days of his apprenticeship and early maturity. This question is one that must be answered individually; my own view is that general standards have deteriorated and that, for example, players have represented Yorkshire in recent years who would not have got a game for the Colts in the 1950s or 1960s.

Ray is an untypical spinner in a number of ways. He likes to bowl with the wind behind him, as opposed to most of his kind who hope that the checking of a ball delivered into the wind will encourage the batsman to misjudge flight; and he is a permanent refutation of the theory that a slow bowler must have large hands in order to spin the ball appreciably. Tom Goddard's right hand before he sent the ball fizzing down the pitch resembled an elevated bucket. Jim Laker's hands and fingers are far larger than the average, but, by comparison, Illy's are small. Yet he spins and has always spun the ball quite enough and is certainly no roller of the ball like the new breed of limited overs 'spinners', who of necessity have to bowl flat and quick to contain the predators. The reason for the first of these unorthodoxies is that as an out-and-out perfectionist Ray is trying to maintain an exact line on or close to the off-stump, an aim which he finds harder to achieve when bowling into the breeze; he has never lost the ability he possessed as a boy to make an out-swinger really go, and on occasions as, to employ Bill Bowes's adjective, a 'miserly' bowler, he flights the ball excellently when bowling to an offside field in the manner of an old-fashioned, slow left-hander.

Lance Gibbs, who recently deprived Ray's old colleague, Fred Trueman, of his record bag of Test victims, was another illustration of distinctive gifts. Exceptionally loose-limbed, he bowled almost on the run, with more than a hint of delivery off the wrong foot. This seemed to allow him readily to vary the speed of arm action relative to body action with consequent subtle variation in flight. Jim Laker, apart from size of hand, possessed abnormal suppleness of wrist. He was a true finger spinner, and his long career in terms of countless overs bowled caused his forefinger to become distended and calloused, with the top two joints bent outwards almost to forty-five degrees; his fierce spin was also achieved by bending the hand back towards the back of the wrist appreciably further than a right angle, so that in addition to the firm tweak imparted to the ball by the fingers the wrist would uncock at delivery like the pecking head of a powerful bird. Illy in physical attributes and technique is by contrast a less distinctive and more orthodox off-spinner.

It would be rash to claim that Ray is a better bowler than either Gibbs or Laker, but surely he must be judged and his talent assessed not only as a bowler but as a true all-rounder, also contributing captaincy of almost the highest calibre and so far ahead of any of his present contemporaries as to make comparison and contrast an embarrassing task.

Certainly in his bowling we find evidence of that intelligent, thoughtful approach that is such a part of the man. In Doug Padgett's words, 'He was a great thinker was Illy.' He knows his limitations. He is not the greatest spinner of the ball, so he has concentrated on spinning it enough and has developed control and accuracy of a standard rarely seen now; a less shrewd cricketer might have striven to spin the ball more vigorously than was natural and failed to develop his full potential owing to lack of length and line. During the 1975 season, in which Leicestershire won their first ever championship, Ray in my opinion was the outstanding spinner in the country. When the ball was biting he was often the match-winner, and though he may not have felt he needed to bowl in the stock role in favourable batting conditions, his value as a limited overs' bowler could hardly be exaggerated. In other words, as a bowler he evinces clear application of intelligence, as he does as a captain and as a batsman. He was and is the thinking man's cricketer, and in no sphere is this more evident than in his concern with physical fitness and meticulous care and preparation for a match. Any spinner's most vulnerable point is his spinning finger and Illy doctors it carefully, painting the crucial point where contact with the ball is most destructive with friar's balsam and carrying with him, to every match, all the medical equipment necessary to deal with any foreseeable problem. This is neither hypochondria nor mere fussiness; it is the application of common sense in order to assure professional efficiency. Certainly there are few if any spinners in the game upon whose accuracy a close fielder can rely with more confidence.

No one is better qualified to assess Ray Illingworth than Jim Binks, who took his bowling for Yorkshire for so many years. His opinion concerning Ray's supremacy might seem odd if one recalls that Fred Titmus was widely regarded as England's number one off-spinner in the early 1960s; Jimmie Binks did not share this view: 'As far as I was concerned, Raymond was the best off-spinner I played with or against. He was one of the hardest to keep to as well, as the variations of his flight were so subtle. He bowled such a good outswinger and with his rather low arm he needed a different technique of keeping. You see, when he wanted to be he was a yard quicker than most. The two basic techniques are — body across with legside taking or hands across without so much body movement. I did the hands across take as I reckon my vision was masked for less long by the body of the batsman. You really had to know Illy's bowling. I reckon I knew when he was going to bowl his seamer as I could see a slight difference of grip and hand position.'

Has Ray Illingworth brought to his batting the same qualities we have discerned in all spheres of his life and thinking? Since his bowling assumed primary importance in his cricket career, there has been a greater feeling of independence of which the all-rounder must be particularly appreciative. Adapting the old golfing adage that 'you drive for fun and putt for money', one can say with regard to Illy that he has often appeared to bat for fun and bowl for money! This is not for a second to denigrate the fighting qualities and essential responsibility of his batting but merely to stress his willingness to 'bat according', as his old mentor Arthur Mitchell would have put it. In fact his readiness to hit the ball in the air when the situation demanded earned him the nickname of 'Slam-Slam' among his Yorkshire teammates in

67

the early 1960s; but even this harmless sobriquet is too flamboyant to be appropriate and he has never been anything else but the dedicated professional, guaranteed as captain or performer to give 100 per cent concentration upon the job in hand.

I suggested earlier that Ray has never quite had the opportunity of developing his batting to its full potential. As soon as he achieved the role of number one off-spinner for Yorkshire, any chance of batting in the first five seemed to depart and, judged on the endless study and practice in which he indulged in his early years to perfect his bowling (comparable with Geoffrey Boycott's titanic labours to hone his batting talents to perfection), Illy's attitude would not have altered if Close or Birkenshaw had been preferred ultimately and he had had to earn his daily bread as a batsman. More probably he would have studied to eliminate error and a less enterprising and exciting batsman might have resulted.

Even as it is, applied experience and thoughtful study have carried him a long way from the eager, inside to out cover-driver who hammered Essex at Hull in 1953 for that glorious 146 not out; had he not developed and adapted his technique, he would not have prospered as he has done. You cannot force on the off-side or cover-drive bowlers who swing, spin or slant the ball in at your leg stump and legs; for every player like Hubert Doggart, essentially an offside player, it seemed that there were ten Doug Insoles, whipping the ball away wide of mid-on, ugly but effective, and the virtue of Illy's batting seems to me that he has largely achieved the crucial facility of the latter without sacrificing the freedom and elegance of the former.

Basically he is an extremely orthodox player in that he swings the bat through the line of the ball, having achieved a balanced striking position by means of a full movement of the feet. We have bred a generation of shufflers and adjusters; several England players in recent years seem to move their front foot no more than eighteen inches when playing forward. Ray's stride with his front foot, like that of most of the really good players that one has watched, is as full as balance and comfort will allow. 'Ticker' Mitchell described the constricted movement as 'batting in a piss-pot', and it is a method that Ray has never adopted. He is also untypical of the present generation of batsmen in that he possesses a full backlift and tends to demonstrate a clear dividing line between attack and defence, rather than employing the graceful half shots that Tom Graveney played with impunity and others use at their peril.

Perhaps, above all, he is a brave batsman. A fine player of the hook shot, he is quick into line and knows where his off-stump is. In 1975 Ray Illingworth at the age of forty-three was one of the best four batsmen in the country, one of whom, Geoff Boycott, refused to play for England; another, Dennis Amiss, was more than a little shell-shocked from the previous winter in Australia, and John Edrich was close on forty. Having said this, it is only logical to add that Illy was in outstanding form during 1975, batting perhaps as well as he has ever done; this surely should have been sufficient reason irrespective of age for his recall to the Test arena, from which he had been banished two years earlier. (A remarkable little story recounted to me by one of the Warwickshire players illustrates the mental torment into which the courageous and free-scoring Amiss had sunk. When testing a new bat, instead of feeling the pick-up as ninety-nine out of a hundred batsmen would have done, he took his stance and instead of picking up the bat went through the motions of ducking a bouncer! I was assured that there was no suspicion of a joke; but it is a source of great pleasure to his many admirers that he managed to struggle his way out of the morass so successfully until the old problems returned in 1977.)

Illy cannot be placed in the very highest class of bowlers, along with, for example, Sydney Barnes, Bill O'Reilly, Jim Laker, Fred Trueman, Wilfred Rhodes, Harold Larwood or Ray Lindwall. Nor obviously can he claim comparable distinction as a batsman with Don Bradman, Peter May, Colin Cowdrey, Len Hutton, the three Ws, Graeme Pollock or Geoff Boycott; who knows whether or not he had the talent and unrealised potential. As a leader, by the very nature of his own psychological make-up, experience and background, it is hard to believe that in terms of pure captaincy he was as great as Frank Worrell, Richie Benaud, Brian Sellers or Walter Robins; but it must be remembered that present-day cricketers possess very different views, attitudes and preconceptions from their predecessors.

If these were 'great' cricketers in their own particular spheres or indeed in a combination of those spheres, then Raymond Illingworth is a 'great' cricketer by aggregate virtue of his skill, dedication, courage, professional efficiency and high level of attainment in all four departments of the game. Since the game achieved its recognisable modern form, it is doubtful that there have been a score to whom he should bow pride of place.

11 Vintage Years Again

When Vic Wilson succeeded Ron Burnet as Yorkshire's captain, he took over a happy and a settled side that was soon to develop into one of the best modern county teams, equipped to dominate all circumstances and conditions. His record was a proud one, two Championship titles out of the three seasons he led the side, but there was a feeling abroad that he should have made it three out of three. Descended from East Riding farming stock, Vic was a good team member who played for his side and a competent captain, but he drew too many matches to escape the charge of being defensively-minded, and in 1961 this cost Yorkshire the Championship, when ten drawn games helped Hampshire to nudge Yorkshire into second place.

If Vic Wilson had a fault it was that he was insufficiently keen to ask or to take advice, but Ray remembers that there had been times in the Yorkshire side when too much advice had been forthcoming from too many folks. At least Wilson avoided the uncertainty that such a state of affairs induces in any captain. An example of the best side of Wilson's approach came over his namesake, the young Don Wilson. The arrival of a new, slow, left-hander in Yorkshire is regarded as comparable with the second coming, and poor Don had been flooded with coaching and counsel good, bad and indifferent until, wholly bewildered, his performance began to suffer. Vic Wilson's reaction was a logical one. He decreed that no one was allowed to advise, coach or help Don with his bowling except Illy, the most knowledgeable and experienced slow bowler in the side.

It was during the 1961 season that Vic, finding that things were not going too well, introduced a curfew. The Yorkshire players had to be in by 11.30 and when Ray heard muffled footsteps along the hotel corridor and observed the surreptitious progress of his captain attempting to reach his bedroom undiscovered by his team-mates at one in the morning, he cheerily called, 'Goodnight, Vic!' He doesn't know to this day whether his voice was recognised!

Certainly Vic Wilson was no nonentity, as his dropping of Fred Trueman at Taunton in 1962 illustrated. Fred arrived late at the ground, after he had received several warnings about lateness; Ray, who suffered the lack of Fred's firepower in the shape of a marauding double century from West Indian Peter Wight, widely regarded as 'Fred's rabbit', supported Vic's decision; he felt that nothing would corrode team spirit more quickly than one law for the star and another for the side's ordinary players. What Vic got wrong was his failure to make clear to the media that Fred had been warned a number of times, so press sympathy was largely transferred from the captain who had to deal with a difficult situation to the culprit who had caused it.

Yorkshire has at most times in its history contributed more than a fair share of forceful, highly articulate and combative competitors to the game. Is it any wonder that a distinctive and effective style of gamesmanship should have been developed and perfected over the years? I use the word 'gamesmanship' advisedly as the Yorkshire 'treatment' was certainly not akin to cheating. When the bowler commenced his run-up the silence would be sufficiently charged with concentrated hostility as to be even more daunting than what had preceded it and would follow it. Business was particularly brisk when, as so often with Yorkshire in the field, the batsman was ringed with a circle of close catchers.

'How much is it turning, Jimmie?'

'Enough.'

'Do you want a man out for him, Raymond?'

'No. He's not a good enough player to hit me there.'

'Don't be making such a big block-hole, lad. You won't be here long enough to use it.'

'Ever had a pair, lad?'

'No.'

'By, it's a lovely day for one.'

And so it would go on, interspersed by the electric silence as the bowler delivered, then on with the chat show again. One particularly effective ploy was to provide the sort of welcome that a batsman detested. Somerset's Australian, Bill Alley, as bluntly uncompromising as any Yorkshireman, was well known to enjoy a chat with all and sundry, so it was the aim of Yorkshire's amateur psychologists to see that no one (but no one) spoke a single word to him, while Dennis Amiss, particularly in his salad days, dearly loved to be left alone to concentrate on the job in hand, so naturally it was the duty of the Yorkshire players to engage him at all possible times in animated conversation.

Something similar to Yorkshire's refined approach could be found in the Surrey side, captained by Stuart Surridge, with the likes of Tony Lock breathing fire and brimstone; and some lively dialogue was always contributed by the Glamorgan team under that gentle and sensitive soul, Wilf Wooller, supported by Haydn Davies behind the stumps. None the less it was generally acknowledged that Yorkshire were masters. Even the Bolshoi and the Beatles had imitators.

It was the colourful and controversial Wilf Wooller who helped to initiate a trend in county cricket that Illy, for one, disapproves of wholeheartedly; the idea that a slow-medium to medium-paced off-spinner like Don Shepherd should have his keeper standing back is anathema to him. The argument is, of course, that stumpings will be rare and catches far more frequent, but the advantage surrendered to the batsman must also be considered. When Ray batted against Shepherd, he used automatically to stand a yard down the pitch when the keeper moved back and regularly nicked the ball when the wicket lacked pace; he survived as it did not carry to the wicket-keeper. 'I reckon they did it basically because the wicket-keepers weren't good enough. Don's quicker one would carry but his stock ball on a slow-turner often wouldn't. If the keeper's standing up to the stumps it limits a batsman. If you've got someone like Knott or Binks over the sticks and you know if you get a leg side half volley and you miss it and lift your foot you've gone, then it's in your mind as you're batting.'

It must not be forgotten that Vic Wilson was Yorkshire's first professional captain; whether or not Lord Hawke, who had died in 1938, actually turned in his grave at the appointment, the contrast with Ronnie Burnet's régime must have been stark. But Vic Wilson's successor, Brian Close, who at the time also appeared to have been appointed because he happened to be senior professional, was a cricketer and a captain of infinitely more talent and potential, the tragedy being that the rich vein of his sheer cricketing ability was only partially worked.

To understand Close one must recall the days of the 'boy wonder' and the blaze of glory that attended his early career. Whereas Illy's career, which has at times been controversial in the extreme, has nevertheless moved upon far more sane and predictable lines, that of Brian Close has fluctuated from crest to trough like the life style of the most pronounced manic depressive. Following his first and only tour of Australia in 1950-1 at the age of nineteen, during which he remembers regularly crying himself to sleep, he returned with confidence apparently shattered and, despite considerable success at both cricket and to a lesser degree at football, continued to swing wildly from an excess to a marked dearth of confidence. Coupled with this, as I have suggested earlier, he seemed to be well on the road to becoming a hypochondriac, and, in fact, during Vic Wilson's short reign, he was warned by his captain that he would have to reconcile himself to a prolonged spell in the second team if he broke down again.

Yet his sheer talent for the game of cricket is so immense that one cannot escape the conclusion that had he been equipped with the temperament, shrewdness, perfectionism and apparently limitless powers of concentration of his old friend and colleague Ray Illingworth he would have approached the incomparable Sobers' brilliance as an all-rounder. But theorising can become tedious; men are as they are.

What is indisputable is that when Brian Close was effectively at the helm, a state of affairs that obtained more rarely in his latter days with Yorkshire, he was a brave and an admirable captain. The trouble was that he could switch off; then a word perhaps from Jimmie Binks ('Hey up, Illy! Rudder's gone again!') and the fact that Brian might be lost in consideration of his last round of golf or his financial problems and had forgotten to change the bowling or field placing would be quietly and unobtrusively corrected. Sometimes, when the problem was at its most acute, it seemed that Brian Close was in a genuine daydream, and Illy recalls one occasion when a gentle bat and pad catch, dollying gently straight to Close at forward short leg, was studiously ignored, while he indulged in a gargantuan yawn.

Again it must be stressed that, during the periods when Brian Close was fully operative, he was a fine captain, positive and imaginative; I have mentioned his courage, the quality for which he became celebrated in the world of cricket, but he was an attacking captain and generally a canny tactician. Whether Ray Illingworth consciously vowed to avoid the errors induced by periodically poor concentration when or if he were allowed the opportunity to lead, I doubt. Certainly yet another in the list of captains who were a formative influence on his own approach to captaincy had registered on the mature Illingworth as vividly as the desirability of a happy dressing-room atmosphere; for Yorkshire in the 1960s was essentially a happy side, despite the inevitable friction resulting from a positive, competitive and ambitious group of men living, playing, travelling and talking together for the best part of seven months every year.

Generally the social life was good too. Once the side was enjoying an uninhibited sing-song in a hotel in Bristol rather later at night than Lord Hawke might have sanctioned and a request came from the management that the festivities should be considerably quietened down; whereupon J. Binks called, in the time-honoured manner of the Music Hall, for: 'Now, lads, one more time with feeling!', and before the next chorus had really got under way the entire Yorkshire contingent found itself out in the street, plus suitcases.

On another occasion at Worksop, the side was split into two hotels, both of which were too small to accommodate the whole party, and the mercurial Binks was again in trouble, having been deprived of the dominoes by a recalcitrant landlady owing to the lateness of the hour. The incident caused the lady in question to pen a letter of complaint to the Yorkshire County Cricket Club concerning the behaviour of Mr Fred Trueman, whose jet black hair she had evidently mistaken for that of Jimmie Binks. Fred was staying at the other hotel. The musical requirements of the side were ably catered for by Messrs Sharpe and Wilson D. who were devoted admirers of the 'Black and White Minstrels', and their contributions were doubtless supplemented by the embryonic stand-up comic act of FST later to be adopted in the night clubs of the north.

During such festivities the captain would giggle away happily when not possessed of a captive audience, and it was no evidence of the dislike or disapproval of his teammates that one of the most popular pastimes was 'teasing Closey'. The virtuoso was unquestionably the dry but witty Doug Padgett, though most of the team had a go at some stage of the proceedings. It was obviously an excellent thing for team spirit that his particular micky could be taken. He had had a reputation for proneness to casualty since his Arsenal days. The manager, observing the uncompromising enthusiasm with which Brian headed the ball high over the bar, had had the Gloucestershire cricketer Arthur Milton, himself an accomplished footballer, crossing the ball from the wing time after time in order to give Brian heading practice; this was so successful that the next match was anticipated with confidence; but the best laid schemes of mice, men and football managers 'gang aft a-gley', and when Milton first crossed the ball there was Brian Close heading downwards so powerfully that the ball struck the ground in front of him and this time shot over the bar first bounce!

Doug Padgett could always get him going on the subject of the time in the services when he had followed Brian at Catterick and had met a certain Sergeant Jones, who, Padgett claimed, had regularly had Close on jankers, scrubbing floors over the weekends, an accusation that used to fill him with real (or simulated) fury so that the offending Padgett would be chased out of the room to the accompaniment of universal mirth. He was never caught.

Close's fury may not normally have lasted long but the storm while it raged used to daunt even the pugnacious Trueman, and the story of one significant clash was widely appreciated on the county circuit. On this particular occasion, Fred had purloined Close's towel, and when it was forcibly reclaimed the intensity of its owner's ire caused Fred to perform one of the fastest and most spectacular streaks, pursued by his captain through the dining area of one county club where those present must have felt that, however impressive the cuisine, it could not quite match up to the standard of the floor show!

Even though he is in his last first-class season as I write, Brian Close, whose incredible array of assorted ailments seemed to depart the moment he was appointed Yorkshire captain, projects an aura of unreality. (Perhaps he has never wholly recovered from the ignominy of dismissal, in his first match for Yorkshire, by the non-deviant, left-handed benevolence of the author!) He was and is an intelligent man; yet he has managed to mask the fact during a long and distinguished career. His talent is indisputable. Possibly he shares with Illy something more than a suspicion of the 'poacher turned gamekeeper'. Both Brian and Ray were keener to impart than to receive discipline. They were more able to evaluate the values of authority when in command than when in subservient roles, and, above all, they found extra qualities and reserves of stamina, intelligence, courage and determination when called upon to lead. The vital difference between the two men was that Ray, as sensitive to background as a chameleon and as dedicated as any Trotskyite, could modify and vary his native bluntness, whereas Brian Close, as admirable a character but a far more vulnerable one, never seemed able to learn how to portray himself (irrespective of the rights and wrongs of an issue) in a favourable light.

12 Tests

Unlike his colleagues Brian Close and Fred Trueman, Illingworth had to graft away patiently as one of a number of potential understudies to Jim Laker, but at last, in July 1958, he was selected for the fourth Test at Manchester. New Zealand had lost the first three and were to lose this by an innings, so that it might be presumed that they were merely grist to the mill, but such a thought would not have troubled the young Illingworth as he drove back over the Pennines, secure at least in the knowledge that he had performed adequately in earning match figures of 3 for 59 in 45 overs, 18 of which were maidens.

Two others, Ted Dexter and Raman Subba Row, also made their débuts with Illy at Manchester, the idea being that they should be scrutinised with selection for the forthcoming tour of Australia in mind. But John Mortimore pipped Ray for the tour as Jim Laker's deputy, though Dexter and Subba Row both made it.

Peter May, one of those rare people who manage to combine courtesy with competitiveness, was the England captain at Old Trafford and made Ray feel at home and part of the team. He has always been sensitive to atmosphere and, pleasantly surprised at May's tough and uncompromisingly 'Yorkshire' attitude on the field following his early years at Charterhouse and Cambridge, Illy became one of his most devoted admirers. Ray was selected for the West Indies tour in the winter of 1959-60 under Peter May. He played in all five Tests and his four Test wickets cost him 95.75 apiece, a fact that did not prevent his captain from making a point of congratulating him on doing an excellent defensive job, adding that he would have liked to have had him in Australia the previous winter. Missed catches, many of them behind the stumps where Roy Swetman did not have the most successful of series, reached double figures off Ray's bowling, and here again it was a confirmatory lesson for him to discover

79

just how little importance Peter May attributed to mere averages viewed out of context.

Apart from his first match against New Zealand, Illy played a couple of home Tests against India in 1959 and enjoyed some success with the bat, his half century at the Oval helping England to an innings victory, after he had scored 162 for Yorkshire against the tourists at Bramall Lane and 21 and 47 not out against them in the fourth Test at Old Trafford; he also played four of the five Tests against South Africa in 1960, though not meeting with particular success.

The truth is that his natural tendency towards insecurity was accentuated by the belief that he was only a stop-gap selection. Playing only odd matches for England, he had little or no chance of demonstrating at this stage that when the ball turned he was the best off-spinner in the country, following Jim Laker's retirement. He rarely seemed able to play as well for his country as he regularly did for Yorkshire.

Ill luck continued to lurk during the 1962-3 Australian tour, crucial to Illy's development in a number of ways. Chosen as a second off-spinner to join Fred Titmus in the fourth Test at Adelaide (Ray himself feels that he should not have been selected owing to the greenness of the wicket), he bowled Bill Lawry through the gate with a little seamer and experienced the chagrin of having Neil Harvey dropped off successive deliveries in the next over, events that are not recorded in the Test averages where one can read the melancholy fact that his one wicket cost him 131 runs. An Australian score of 21 at the fall of the third wicket (Brian Statham had dismissed Bobbie Simpson, caught behind) and a personal return at that stage of 2 for 0 would have done England and Illingworth no harm at all.

Despite disappointing figures with both bat and ball (before some batting success in the later games against New Zealand) Ted Dexter's tour, under the management of the Duke of Norfolk, was an important milestone for Illy.

Several indelible lessons were learnt and they were not flattering to the establishment, though he acknowledges the efficiency and dedication of Alec Bedser, who was the Duke's assistant manager. There was a wide gulf between the amateur and professional cricketers, so that the touring party seemed to him to be drastically split. Nets were too often poorly organised and, perhaps above all, he felt that the wrong sides were selected for particular matches given the type of wicket at different venues. When, at team meetings, general discussion was invited, Ray characteristically spoke his mind, especially on the subject of team selection, and he firmly believes that the fact that his tour bonus was halved stems from nothing more reprehensible than his frank talking. One other event may have contributed. One of the earliest causes of friction between Illingworth and Cowdrey was the latter's tendency to turn up late for net practice so that bowlers who had done their stint were required to go on bowling in order to accommodate the late arrival. Illy might not have realised that Colin Cowdrey's duties as vice-captain were the cause of his lateness, and on one occasion resentment boiled over into a firm verbal assault; sadly, the seeds of antipathy had been sown.

When Ray returned from this tour and it became known that his bonus had been halved to £50, Sir William Worsley, president of the Yorkshire County Cricket Club, asked him if he would like a hearing, as no reason for the punishment had been given (and has not till this day been given). Dates for meetings were several times suggested but on each and every occasion the Duke of Norfolk was unavailable. Over this incident and many more, one comes back to the basic fact of trust. When versions of a story differ, whom is one to believe? I have taxed Ray uncompromisingly on this subject and can only say that I, for one, believe his story to be true. Being the man he is, Illy's opinion that the Duke of Norfolk was little more than a likeable and impressive figurehead would not have remained hidden for long. He did not enjoy his 'disgrace' but as far as he was concerned his conscience was clear and he was confirmed, if confirmation had been needed, in the view that a captain must whenever remotely possible support and represent his players, rather than appear to them to be an extended limb of the establishment. Ted Dexter was an enigma. Ray unequivocally admits that he likes and liked him as a man; but those of us who have seen him practising his golf swing while his duties as captain seemed to demand tactical manoeuvring or who know the story of the Sussex side under his captaincy trooping off the field with nine of the opposition's wickets down to listen to a transistor broadcast of a famous race, under the unconvincing pretext of taking drinks, will realise that he possessed more than a little of the Don Quixote.

Now the grapevine bore the damaging news that 'of course, Illingworth is a bad tourist.' Passed over by the England selectors in the West Indies series in 1963 and for the Indian tour in 1964, he was also ignored for the MCC tour of South Africa in 1964-5 under Mike Smith but played one Test against the New Zealanders in the summer of 1965. It was only with the appointment of Brian Close to the England captaincy in 1967 that his real merit was recognised, and even this year, one of triumphant success, was marred before its close.

Suddenly the luck had changed and he found himself called to bowl not once but several times in Test matches where the ball would bite. Illy's figures for the three match series against India make interesting reading: his match analysis at Leeds was 7 for 131 off 80 overs and second innings figures of 6 for 29 on a rain-affected wicket at Lord's followed to win both bowling awards made by Horlicks Ltd, though Robin Hobbs was preferred in the third and last Test at Birmingham, although he had match figures inferior to Ray's, presumably to share the goodies round a bit.

When rejoining the Yorkshire side following the first Test against Pakistan the same summer, he was told by his captain, 'the England selectors are trying out another off-spinner for the second Test.' He was hurt and surprised; but he could hardly believe his ears when he discovered it was his old friend and rival, Fred Titmus, virtually the same age and veteran of innumerable Tests. What smarted above all was that his own county captain, Brian Close, had apparently not fought for his retention. A glance at *Wisden* will confirm that Illy's fury was understandable; he still finished comfortably head of the joint bowling averages for the two three-match series, taking five more wickets than any other England bowler, despite the fact that he missed the last two matches. If the young and promising Pat Pocock had been preferred at this stage for the reasons given, the whole depressing incident would have become explicable and therefore more tolerable. Even this insult to his professional pride and ability was soon forgiven if not forgotten. Both he and Brian Close got down to helping Yorkshire to their sixth Championship victory in nine years, though the manner in which it was won with regard to one match in particular was bound to cause considerable controversy and resulted in Close losing the England captaincy for the forthcoming tour of the West Indies.

The 'time-wasting' incident occurred at Edgbaston in August. Illy was playing in this match and comes down firmly in Brian Close's defence. 'I don't think there was any deliberate time-wasting. There was a lot of talk about the last over which Fred bowled but he bowled a couple of no balls and a wicket fell. It certainly was a bloody long time. I didn't know till after we came off the field that Fred had bowled the no balls on purpose, so to that extent I suppose it was deliberate. He'd wanted to be sure that his was the last over. Actually the umpire didn't call one of them. Our own press criticised us and being a facts and figures man I took figures to them in the next two matches. Our over rate in the first hour of both matches was the same as it had been at Edgbaston. Another thing you must remember is that it was a sopping wet outfield with spray shooting up each time the ball ran over the ground so that we were entitled to stop every ball and dry it by the umpire, instead of drying it on the way back to our mark as we did. We played near one side of the ground so that the ball had to be fetched back around a hundred and thirty yards every time it went to the boundary and we had Fred bowling off his long run with another seamer the other end. Thirteen overs an hour isn't great but it's what we normally bowled when we were trying to bowl a side out.'

The crux of the matter is whether or not Brian Close instructed Fred Trueman to bowl the no balls or whether he did it on his own initiative. Certainly if the latter is the case it explains the Vesuvian eruption of fury on the part of Brian Close immediately after the match and the proximity to demolition experienced by one particular Warwickshire supporter.

In the end the two points squeezed from this match proved to be irrelevant. Yorkshire finished ten points ahead of Kent and Leicestershire, after they had beaten Gloucestershire at Harrogate on the last day of the season. Illy was virtually unplayable, taking 7 for 6 to add to his return of 7 for 58 in the first innings. Outstanding form of this calibre eventually regained Ray his England place in 1968 against the Australians, and it must have been a great disappointment to him that second-innings bowling figures of 6 for 87 off 51 overs at Headingley, in the face of dour defensive batting, did not manage to win the match and keep alive England's hopes of regaining the Ashes.

Brian Close's brief reign as England's captain had, of course, begun at the Oval in 1966. Driving down to London, Illy had several times pressed Close to ask the England quickies to give Gary Sobers a bouncer early on, and, following his fine 81 in the first innings, Sobers became the real danger man after the England attack had shot out the cream of the West Indies early batting. What happened is history. Snow duly obliged with a particularly vicious bouncer. Sobers mis-hooked and there was Close, unlike many short legs who would have been flat on their faces praying for survival, erect and alert to take the simple catch that dollied off the great man's glove. The whole contest, including the interviews that the England captain gave on the subject of 'the plan we had to get rid of Sobers', pointed once again to the inexaggerable part that luck can play in any sports-man's career and above all in that of a Test captain. Without the heroic exploits of John Snow and Ken Higgs, who added 128 in a last wicket stand that finished two short of the world record, and the fact that John Murray also chose this match to bat like an angel, Close would never have possessed the luxury of a position of extreme strength from which to dictate to one of the strongest Test sides of modern times.

To those of us who admire and respect Brian Close (and that is not the same thing as pretending that his faults do not exist), there is an element of sadness about what then seemed certain to be the end of his Test career; but perhaps the greatest compli-ment that one can pay him is to acknowledge the defensive skill and courage with which he met the hostile battery of West Indian pace, spearheaded by Andy Roberts, when recalled to the

Test arena in 1976 at the age of forty-five.

It is depressing to those with the best interests of English cricket at heart that for too long the captaincy has been awarded primarily by default. Close erred or, as many Yorkshiremen still think, was believed to have erred, and the captaincy went to Colin Cowdrey, a great batsman but hardly a dynamic leader. In 1969 a number of strong contenders disappeared from the scene for varying reasons, and Ray Illingworth was appointed. Soon a new candidate had been promoted, Mike Denness, whose régime ended when it was realised that he was neither a good enough player when the heat was on nor a sufficiently positive leader; Tony Greig was installed in 1976, with optimistic hallelujahs, in an office for which he was transparently not then ready, and Mike Brearley's appointment followed Greig's fall from grace.

13 Yorkshire's Loss

In 1961 under Vic Wilson at Hull an incident occurred that Illy was to remember seven years later when his departure from Yorkshire was imminent. He had suffered a slight strain in the area of his ribs while batting but with evidence of turn in the wicket had bowled, and his return of 5 for 51 had helped Yorkshire to a nine wickets victory; but the injury had been aggravated. He played in the next two matches with the injury strapped and in considerable discomfort but missed the Somerset game at Taunton and after rest and treatment reported at Bradford where Yorkshire were playing Sussex. Illy ran round the ground three or four times, bowled and batted hard at the nets and judged after this extensive work-out that he was fit to play in the current match. At this point Brian Sellers arrived and after Illy had informed him that he was fit, Sellers said, 'you'll be all right for the second team match next Wednesday then.'

This was on a Saturday morning and, in the belief that Yorkshire had eleven fit men at the ground, Sellers departed to the dressing room to discover that one of the eleven had declared himself unfit and that therefore Ray was required after all. Back he came. 'Nah then. Are you fit to play?'

'I'm bloody not. I wouldn't play for you if it was the last game in the country.'

Shortly after Ronnie Burnet, then a member of the Yorkshire committee, arrived and asked, 'Are you fit?'

'Yes.'

'Will you play?'

'Not for him.'

'Will you play for me?'

And, of course, Illy played and played well, helping Yorkshire to a crucial win. What is so significant surely is that the injury that had lost him match money and occasioned the brush with Sellers had been sustained while he had been loyally serving his employers, the Yorkshire County Cricket Club, under difficult circumstances. Is it any wonder with treatment like this in mind that so many players of his generation held the view that they won the Championship in spite of, and not because of, the committee?

In the season of 1968 Yorkshire won their seventh championship in ten years and heading their bowling averages with twenty wickets at 10.55 apiece was a young off-spinner called Geoff Cope. He had made his début for the county in 1966 without taking a wicket but in the following season had also headed the averages, taking thirty-two wickets at 12.78 each. No wonder with the geriatric Illingworth knocking on towards forty there was muttering. The fact that informed opinion in the side held that if Cope got 6 for 50 on a turner Illy would have got 8 for 30 was apparently disregarded. No one could have known at this stage of his career that Ray's best years were still to come.

It may have been the knowledge or suspicion that there was a pro-Cope and therefore, by implication at least, an anti-Illingworth lobby on the committee that caused Ray, in his thirty-seventh year, to be acutely aware of the need for security in what he then regarded as the evening of his career; he re-opened the question of a contract as opposed to the 'gentlemen's agreement' between club and players which in practical terms meant a month's notice from either party for release or dismissal. Again in practice requests for release were often refused whereas obviously notice of dismissal, as in any other sphere, had to be accepted. In fairness there were two sides to this question. Prior to the granting of contracts to Yorkshire players, the county probably felt more obligation to help a player whom they had sacked. Paternalism combined with self-interest in the case of Bob Appleyard, whose treatment for tuberculosis in Switzerland was paid for by the county club, and the popular Cyril Turner was considerably helped during a troublesome period of illness; but, quite apart from the fact that the sixteen other counties all gave contracts, there seems to be no doubt to modern eyes that the 'gentlemen's agreement' principle was wrong and Ray Illingworth was right. Within months of his leaving the club for Leicestershire capitulation had occurred and the principle of contracts accepted.

The crisis was precipitated by a visit to John Nash, the Yorkshire secretary, in which Illy asked if it were true that Geoff Cope was going to be pushed in front of him. 'If so,' he said, 'that's okay. Give me my release and I'll be happy to go. But please don't mess me about for a year and then sack me when I've missed the chance of getting a three- or four-year contract with somebody else.' John Nash denied that there was any chance of Ray's fears proving to be reality, but he was far from convinced. Eventually he was assured that the committee would never grant him a contract. The fateful letter was written and at once released to the press by Sellers before the committee had had any chance of discussion or possible modification of their views.

It was during a match at Bradford that Bill Bowes arrived in the Yorkshire dressing-room and asked Ray if it was correct that he was leaving. Illy's reaction was immediate. 'How the hell do you know? The letter's only been in half-an-hour.'

'Mr Nash has rung Sellers and Sellers says that you can go and any bugger else that wants to can go with you. He's asked me to handle the press side of things.'

Feelings were sufficiently high on the subject of contracts for several of the senior players to say that they would back Ray to the extent of not playing under certain circumstances. The whole unsavoury affair certainly ended happily for its principal participant but with the somewhat tarnished image of democracy further dented in the county club. It was not as if this was the only time that Sellers acted without the authority of his committee; one was left with the feeling that a high percentage of committee members were thoroughly in awe of him so that what he said was law.

The basic point was that Illy's letter of 'resignation' was conditional upon the committee's final decision to refuse him the contract and the security he demanded. In fact that decision was made by one autocratic individual with whom Ray had on at least one occasion rowed more or less violently and who appeared to be backing a less experienced bowler, prematurely, to usurp his place. It is perfectly possible that the committee, if they had seen that Illingworth and those senior players (Boycott,

Trueman and Close among them who supported him whole-heartedly) really meant business, would have reconsidered their refusal to give contracts; but they had been utterly pre-empted by Sellers.

As soon as the news of Ray Illingworth's departure from Yorkshire became public, his real value could be judged by the number of offers he received from league clubs and counties; what was so amazing to him was that several league clubs were willing to pay him more for weekend cricket than he had been receiving from Yorkshire for the long hard graft of a full season.

Perhaps it was understandable in the official version of the drama that the committee could not 'allow a pistol to be held to its head', but surely the really iniquitous factor was that the committee was effectively not allowed in a crisis concerning the county's and the country's leading all-rounder to fashion the club's policy. Leicestershire smiled broadly and opened its arms to a player who the very season of his resignation had averaged close on thirty with the bat; no English all-rounder was above him in the batting averages and he finished fourth in the first-class bowling averages as the country's leading wicket-taker. Many keen, devoted Yorkshire cricket fans to whom I spoke then and have spoken since saw Illy's departure as the crowning condemnation of the blinkered policies that had too often seemed to motivate crucial decisions. Close's head was soon to roll — but that is another and a more intelligible story.

14 Captaincy

Illy is a player's player and it followed logically that he became a player's captain. Nor surprisingly those who have played under him are generally appreciative of the fact that he has looked after their interests and avoided the old gulf that could develop when it was felt that the captain was representing merely the interests of the club.

Perhaps he was fortunate to be given the opportunity to captain so late in his own successful career. When he led the Leicestershire side out onto the Grace Road turf on 10 May 1969, he had not captained a side in first-class cricket a dozen times and had rarely captained at any level since his youth at Farsley. He had known leadership of wildly differing attitude and approach. He had suffered in a disaffected side; he had enjoyed playing in a happy one, and he had discovered that the latter breeds success. Confident in the mature efficiency of his own all-round performance, he could still recall the days when he had known what it was to struggle. All he wanted from a player under him was 100 per cent effort and concentration.

It would have been surprising if a man of his intelligence had not learnt from the strengths and weaknesses of Norman Yardley, Billy Sutcliffe, Ronnie Burnet, Vic Wilson and Brian Close, not to mention the captains under whom he had played Test cricket. He is a hard man but those who know him best regard him as a fair and a straight one. Moreover he knows the game of cricket as well as any and a computer-like registration of an opponent's frailties, combined with an endless willingness to fiddle and manipulate field placing and bowling changes to discomfort or dismiss a troublesome batsman, has made him a formidable captain.

He remembered well that in his early Test matches he had received the impression that he was only a stand-in, chosen for reasons of convenience rather than as a real mark of recognition;

91

consequently he had never really felt himself to be a secure member of the side. Thus, in the crucial sphere of man-management, he was far more aware of the pitfalls possible than a younger and less battle-scarred warrior. Not all those who have played under Illy have liked him; he would, I suspect, regard mere liking as irrelevant. More to the point, they have respected him as a cricketer and a leader. Many captains have been inextricably associated with the establishment of the game; some, having come up from the ranks, may have fallen into the opposing error of failing to achieve the independence necessary for the job through always trying to be one of the boys. It is a captain's duty to make decisions and it is inevitable that some will be unpopular.

He had become progressively more confident in the face of the demands made upon him by the media and had learned, ignoring the advice given him by Len Hutton years ago in the Yorkshire side, that the vast majority of journalists react favourably to frank and open treatment. He had become a competent public speaker, though never a devoted one, and he had learned the art of projecting a favourable image, where once stubbornness or shyness might have intervened. He seemed, it might appear, 'armed at all points', but there was an exception. To his critics or enemies, Ray Illingworth seems to have a chip on his shoulder. It would be surprising if he did not, but, though the chip itself may be trivial enough, it does carry with it a basic problem to which a more diplomatic, less forthright person would readily find a solution.

Earlier I quoted Fred Trueman's opinion that Illy was basically lacking in confidence; the young Yorkshire all-rounder may certainly have lacked confidence, but the England captain surely did not. The intensity of his dedicated professionalism was bound to focus his irritation and attention almost exclusively on the immediate slight or problem. When an objective assessment was required, Illy, an able tactician, too often proved himself to be a limited strategist: thus his critics might argue in the context of his recovery of the Ashes in 1970-1 that he won the battle but came close to losing the war. When he believed himself firmly in the right in the face of what he regarded as ignorance, injustice or prejudice there was little room for debate, and on occasions this lack of flexibility has drawn him into error no less real because it was provoked. An example, of course, was the Lou Rowan/John Snow confrontation mentioned in more detail earlier, but the point must be made that the degree of anger that Ray evinced on one well-publicised occasion alone did avoidable harm at a number of levels. If an England captain is seen apparently gibbering with fury at an umpire's decision (or indeed lack of decision) then by direct implication it is the idea of authority that is being questioned. It is not enough to behave impeccably until something occurs that infuriates you.

Secondly, the vast number of viewers at a ground or watching on television makes the opportunity for the exercise of good or bad influence, especially upon the young, immensely more potent; a youngster sees his favourite footballer lash out, kick wildly or scream abuse or an admired and famous rugby player strike an opponent off the ball or rake him with his studs in a ruck, and the likelihood of that young person's becoming dedicated to the highest standards of sportsmanship and behaviour has been greatly reduced.

Is this a harsh view of Illy? It is not that he was in the wrong but that on several isolated occasions he put himself in the wrong by over-reaction and loss of control: he could still blow his top, and that particular activity is fraught with danger for anyone in the public eye.

The only other significant criticism that might be made with regard to Ray's captaincy is the one levelled by his great friend and admirer, Jimmie Binks, that he could be negative in his attitude. The words Jim actually used were, 'Closey had flair but Raymond could be rather negative.' A man's strengths and weaknesses are closely linked. If Brian Close had had less flair and more keen, directed intelligence and common sense he would have avoided some of the errors and misfortunes from which he has suffered. If Ray had not been a meticulous thinker and planner, a man whose concentration would rarely if ever flag, he would doubtless have been more likely to adopt an imaginative, unpredictable or unorthodox approach. Both Close and Illingworth are admirable but different individuals and the praiseworthy side of the coin is clearly inscribed; the other is that Close, for his part, could periodically switch off and apparently forget his duties as a captain and that Illy could be guilty of the charge laid by Jimmie Binks.

Yet Illingworth is not essentially a defensive or negative cricketer or captain, a fact that he demonstrated on his arrival at Leicester. Too many drawn matches are often evidence that the captain's declarations have been too harsh and that he has been unwilling to chase an opponent's declared total. When Warwickshire finished the 1971 season as runners-up to Surrey they had lost nine matches, won nine and only drawn six, while poor Derbyshire, languishing at the foot of the Championship table, had only managed one win, four losses and nineteen draws. Generally speaking the two Smiths, Alan and Mike, his vice-captain, had set feasible targets when they declared and had gone for feasible targets when set them, while Derbyshire, up to their eyes in gloom, had far too often settled for a draw with a muttered prayer of thanksgiving that it had not been a defeat! In Illy's first season at Leicester, 1969, they finished fourteenth in the table having been second at the end of May. Ray, in fine form with both bat and ball, finished top of both the county's batting and bowling averages but had to miss nine Championship matches for Test matches during which the slide began; the final table showed that they had won four matches, lost seven and drawn thirteen, as opposed, for example, to Lancashire's record of two wins, one loss and a staggering twenty-one drawn games under Jack Bond. Lancashire finished only one place lower in the table than Leicestershire!

Yorkshire, most fair-minded people would agree, enjoyed a deal more than their quota of good luck in 1975 to finish as championship runners-up to Leicestershire, drawing nine matches and only losing one. The nagging suspicion remained that, irrespective of relative merit when judged against the other contenders, if Geoff Boycott had instructed Yorkshire to go boldly for a win in half a dozen of the nine matches they drew they would have won two or three more and lost two or three more, with the rest, if any, still drawn. But of, course, so might Leicestershire, who also only lost one match; both Boycott and

Illingworth would recall the magic word 'Hove' though only the latter was playing in the match in question, which still serves as a salutary reminder that in cricket use of the word 'impossible' should be kept to an absolute minimum.

If judged upon a certain number of the drawn games referred to above, Illy's captaincy might be regarded as cautious; but equally, if one recalls, for example, his third match as England's new captain in 1969, he is triumphantly vindicated. This was the game above any other that Illy feels was his *tour de force* as a captain, though he is quick to add that, as so often, luck played its considerable part. Perhaps the greatest compliment he received was that after the match the West Indian players said to several of the England team, 'If Cowdrey had captained England in this match, there's no way that England could have won.' Ironically, Illy's opportunity to captain England had come with Cowdrey's injury to his achilles tendon in May. He missed all six Tests that summer.

It was a low-scoring match at Headingley in July, in which overcast conditions for much of the time plus a green wicket made batting difficult; the West Indian seamers put England out for 223 but Barry Knight, spearheading a keen seam attack, still earned England a lead of 62; again no one really dominated in the second innings and it needed a sterling tail end 34 from David Brown, well supported by Knight and Derek Underwood, to set West Indies 303 to win with the time factor clearly irrelevant. It was one of those matches when the Headingley pitch grew easier and, West Indies having reached over 200 for 3, they must have been clear favourites to square the rubber. Asked his opinion after the match, Basil D'Oliveira did not share this view. 'Even though they'd reached that score,' he said, 'I always felt that Ray was in control.'

After John Snow had sent back Roy Fredericks, Underwood accounted for the principal run-makers, Camacho and Butcher, before Knight dismissed Sobers, driving wildly before he was set. A feature of the series was the 'Sobers plan'. Ray decreed that his apparent vulnerability to a wide half-volley early on must be exploited, and in Knight they had the man to do this. Sobers was caught in the slips by Sharpe in the first innings and bowled, doubtless bent on vengeance, in the second. Now Ray had a problem. Clive Lloyd is the sort of player who can swing a close match in a single over and, with Underwood turning in to him as a left-hander, slaughter might have resulted. His decision could hardly be faulted in terms of positive thinking. He came on himself, though Underwood was clearly not too happy about being taken off when he was among the wickets. The move worked, and when Clive Lloyd was caught behind off Illingworth Underwood was back on at once with the match virtually won and lost. Every move Ray had tried at Headingley had come good and, having helped to save a sickly situation with his maiden Test century in the second Test at Lord's, with the first safely won, this crushing victory at Leeds did much to confirm his claim to the England captaincy; with the future in mind what was even more important than the actual result was the strong feeling among the players that a hard, shrewd professional cricketer, with their interests and the winning of every match at heart, was now at the helm.

Illy's impressive form with the bat continued at Lord's where he led England to a massive 230-run victory over New Zealand in the second half of the 1969 season, contributing a half century in the first innings; the ball turned from the match's early stages and he was top scorer in England's indifferent total of 190, before Derek Underwood and Ray in the first innings and Underwood, irresistible in the second, swept New Zealand to defeat. Rain ruined the second test at Nottingham but the England attack in the first innings proved too much for the tourists and Illy could look back on his first season as England's captain with the reassuring record of four wins and two drawn games out of the two three-match series.

A winter without cricket was followed by the unhappy cancellation of the South African tour and the hasty filling of the vacuum by the glamorous 'Rest of the World' series, during which Ray reached a confidence and consistency with the bat he has never before or since approached in the face of comparable opposition; only Sobers scored more runs. The Rest's attack makes formidable reading. Sobers, McKenzie, Barlow, Procter and Intikhab all played as well as Gibbs, whose three wickets from four matches incredibly cost him 102.33 runs apiece.

The series started disastrously for England, but Illy followed 63 in the first knock out of a total of 127, with a superb 94 in the second innings, though defeat was still by as much as an innings and 80 runs. The bowling of Basil D'Oliveira and Tony Greig and another sterling knock from Ray, bowled by Sobers three short of his century, helped England to victory at Trent Bridge, and the sides met at Birmingham just over a week later, where the captaincy of the winter tour of Australia and New Zealand was to be announced. England got a real mauling from the West Indians in the middle order, supplemented by the hugely talented Mike Procter, but still fought well to take the match into the last hour, losing by five wickets. When Illy was bowled by Lance Gibbs after a defensive dogfight of over two hours, he came back into the pavilion to be met by Alec Bedser. He took off his pads, had a quick wash and joined Bedser in the umpire's room where he was told that 'we would like you to take the side to Australia and we'd like Colin to be vice-captain.' Understandably delighted at the invitation and having concentrated fiercely on his batting for the previous two hours, it was clearly impossible for Ray to give an objective and considered opinion on the vice-captaincy; hindsight suggests that it was a package deal, designed by the selectors to placate Colin Cowdrey who had been passed over for the leadership. Perhaps this was an example of a typical British compromise that merely guaranteed future problems. Rumour at the time suggested that Alec Bedser had voted against Illingworth's appointment but, as soon as the decision was made, Bedser showed himself more than ready to accept it and co-operate, while Colin Cowdrey's friends and admirers were incensed. ('How disgracefully poor Colin's been treated' and 'Colin would have got the job if *he'd* lived in a semi-detached house in Bradford. He shouldn't go.') What was apparently forgotten was that Cowdrey's superb batsmanship was not in question but that Illy had convinced the selectors that he was the better and more decisive captain.

It is impossible not to feel sympathy for Cowdrey. Motivated in his long and illustrious career by a deep and disinterested love of cricket rather than by mere glory-seeking, he still had one ambition. He had never led an MCC tour to Australia and the stark realisation that he would never fulfil this ambition inevitably resulted in frustrated disappointment; but if he had been able to act more decisively in accepting or rejecting the vice-captaincy it is possible that the tour would have got off to a smoother start. In fact it took him about a week to make up his mind, during which time he was prompted by a letter from Illy urging him to forget any differences that they may have had and to help to make the tour a success. There was still a time-lag between Cowdrey's eventual, reluctant acceptance of the vice-captaincy and the arrival of the letter, so that on reflection Illy feels that it would have been better for all parties if the offer of the vice-captaincy had been withdrawn in the light of Colin Cowdrey's obvious doubt and reluctance.

If he had eventually refused the offer or if it had been withdrawn, Ray's own choice for the vice-captaincy might well have radically altered the recent history of English Test cricket. It would have been Geoff Boycott, whom he believes would have found the eventual task of captaining ten mature international cricketers in Test matches less demanding than the day to day problems of man-management facing a county captain. Ray feels, moreover, that Geoff Boycott's withdrawal from Test cricket was largely motivated by a desire to prove himself as a captain. However illogical, the idea that 'Boycott is a bad captain because Yorkshire have not done well' has been expressed, though one has never heard the same twisted thinking applied to Tony Greig and Sussex; but the one single factor that accounted for Yorkshire's finishing as runners-up to Leicestershire in the 1975 championship was surely Boycott's own phenomenal success with the bat. Whether or not Geoff Boycott will ever now get the chance to captain England must be very doubtful, but those who put forward a case for his pre-eminence as a leader on the evidence of the 1975 season must expect a verdict of 'not proven'.

After the Edgbaston 'Test' against the Rest of the World, which might so easily have been saved, England had a real chance of winning the fourth 'Test' at Leeds; with a half century in each innings Illy helped to fight England to a situation from which victory at one time seemed probable. Needing 223 to win the match and the series on a good wicket, the Rest faltered in the face of fine bowling from John Snow and Ray Illingworth. With both Rohan Kanhai and Barry Richards injured they commenced the last day at 75 for 5, but Sobers and Intikhab first fought, then hit their side into a commanding position. After Sobers was caught at slip off Snow, the greatest batsman in the world, Barry Richards, came in at number ten and he and Mike Procter, with only Lance Gibbs to follow, took the Rest of the World to victory in a wonderful match that could so easily have gone the other way.

Ray's last knock of the series at the Oval was a duck, but his first-innings half century in a match that the Rest won by four wickets left him second in the England batting averages, having scored 476 runs at an average of 52.88 with every innings completed.

15 And So To Australia

In *Wisden's* account of the 1970-1 tour, E. M. Wellings, whose admiration for Illy's leadership is transparent, wrote, 'No captain of a touring team since D. R. Jardine nearly 40 years ago has had such a difficult task as Raymond Illingworth,' and he goes on to express the crux of the matter in the words, 'Some English critics, who had championed the cause of M. C. Cowdrey, were against the skipper.' Virtually as soon as the MCC landed, it was apparent that there was, as in Ray's first tour of Australia under the Duke of Norfolk, a potential split in the touring party. The manager, David Clark, a transparently likeable and conscientious man, tried desperately hard initially to bridge the psychological gap but temperamentally and in background he was far closer to Cowdrey than to Illingworth.

Cowdrey himself did not seem anxious to share the day-to-day responsibilities of the tour with Ray and to their credit, seeing the pressure under which Illy daily found himself, Geoff Boycott and John Edrich offered and proceeded efficiently to organise the practice sessions; but for his part Cowdrey may well have experienced a degree of coldness from his senior colleagues and on one occasion actually said ruefully to David Clark, 'I'm just not wanted.'

The sheer weight throughout the tour of attention from the media was immediately apparent; Illy recalls that the 'plane carrying the touring party flew over Adelaide at ten o'clock in the morning, landed in Sydney and then returned to Adelaide at three o'clock in the afternoon. During the first break at Sydney, Ray was hauled off into a tiny room where a twenty-minute press conference was held with questions flying like machine-gun bullets; the fact that, then and thereafter, he tried whenever possible to give frank and positive answers to fair questions must have helped to foster the generally good relationship that he enjoyed with the vast majority of Australian pressmen. Ray is, at his own admission, far from the best traveller in the world and

101

he found the experience, following a long and tiring journey, more than a little daunting.

On his arrival exhausted at Adelaide, there were, predictably, more interviews at the airport, and when they reached the hotel Ray asked David Clark if he was then free and was assured that he was. An hour later he was woken from a deep sleep by his room phone ringing. 'Could Mr Illingworth please come to the manager's room?' The impression that he gained was that the press were not getting enough out of David Clark and wanted to try their hand with the tour captain. Soon the 'wise' phrases were rolling off the conveyor-belt and it was not long before Ray was back in his bed, after receiving warm protestations of gratitude from the journalists whose columns could now be filled with deathless prose concerning 'two of the fastest bowlers in the world in John Snow and Alan Ward. I think they'll bowl great out here,' a pronouncement that approached the prophetic at least in the case of Snow.

When the cricket started the pressures obviously mounted rather than decreased. The press saw Illingworth every day of the tour, at the end of which he was thanked by a large contingent for being 'the most frank and straightforward captain ever to tour Australia'. He may have failed to achieve rapport with a section of the English press who never managed to accept that he had been awarded the captaincy ahead of Cowdrey, but his relationship with the Australian press was excellent during a rubber, moreover, that their country lost, and with it the Ashes.

Another misconception that must be cleared up before dealing with the actual cricket and some of the stormy incidents it provoked is that the basic relationship between the two sides was bad on this tour. This was not the case. Generally there was far less swearing on the field than has since become the accepted rule, and during every Test match when the day's play was done several members of both sides would sit talking and enjoying a beer and each other's company for as long as a couple of hours after the close. Surely this is one of the most vital constituents of sport at any level if it is to fulfil its most important function of uniting rather than dividing people. Ray and the Aussies would cheerfully have cut each other's metaphorical throats on the field, but afterwards there was chat, discussion, anecdote and discord resolved into harmony. It was Illy's contention that when facing hard opponents he had to be (and to be seen to be) as hard as they, but this was not an approach, contrary to the belief of some of his critics, that he maintained after the day's last ball was bowled.

There were further and fairly widespread charges of bad manners and even rudeness. (On one occasion Illy was unwise enough to inspect the wicket prior to an important match attired in bedroom slippers!) In this context, if the management and the vice-captain had been closer to the captain and senior players, it is likely that general diplomacy and over-commitment to a plethora of social functions might have been shared more equally; on the other hand it is impossible to escape the conclusion that Ray Illingworth himself and several others, John Edrich and Geoff Boycott among them, should also have worked harder to bridge the gap of temperament and background that caused the rift. Personal feelings would have been irrelevant. They would have been putting themselves last and the tour and therefore English cricket first. Neither side was able to budge from its entrenched position and to that extent both were to some degree surely at fault.

England went into the first Test at Brisbane with three drawn games and a defeat in the major matches to their 'credit' and did well to fight back after a double century from Ken Stackpole, who had received the benefit of the doubt from umpire Lou Rowan at the commencement of his marathon innings when photographic evidence clearly proved that the run out decision should have gone the other way. That England led Australia's total of 433 by 31 was highly creditable and it was during this first innings of the first Test that Illy failed with the bat for the only time in the seven match series.

Following the second Test at Perth, also drawn, during which Illy and umpire Rowan had failed to agree upon the correct definition of a bouncer, the third Test, scheduled for Melbourne, was abandoned without a ball being bowled; a one-day fixture was played instead on the last day, which the Australians won comfortably, so that the sides met at Sydney with MCC having only won one first-class match, that against modest opposition in Tasmania. Seeds of dissension were growing because of a pronouncement to pressmen by David Clark, following the Perth Test, that 'we need some positive and challenging tactics in the Tests.' When asked whether he would prefer to see the next four Tests drawn or for Australia to win them three-one, he replied, 'I'd rather see four results.' These remarks were perhaps wrongly interpreted by the touring party as an attack on them and it was from this time that David Clark's relationship with many of the MCC team, especially Ray Illingworth, deteriorated. Those who know David Clark would be in no doubt that his remarks were motivated not by animosity but by a simple wish that the tour should be a success and the touring party's image be undamaged.

The fourth Test at Sydney was a triumph for the three key tourists. Illy batted well and captained the side with characteristic skill; John Snow bowled with fire and accuracy to earn second innings figures of 7 for 40 and Geoff Boycott contributed 219 runs for once out in a match that England won by 299 runs to swing the rubber sharply their way.

The fifth Test at Melbourne was drawn, eight dropped catches in the first innings easing Australia's task. But a worrying foretaste of the troubles still ahead was provided by a stampede of about two thousand spectators, most of them children, to congratulate Ian Chappell on his first Test hundred against England. Also Snow was warned for over-use of the bouncer during Australia's second innings, this time by umpire O'Connell.

Generally the reception given to the England side and its captain, who was booed on several occasions when he came out to bat during the latter part of the tour, clearly illustrated the mounting tension that was to flare so vigorously in the second Sydney Test.

Controversy again intruded in the sixth Test at Adelaide when Geoff Boycott, believing himself to have been wrongly adjudged run out by umpire O'Connell, threw down his bat in petulant anger. When the question of an apology was discussed the line Boycott took was, 'I'll apologise but I'll tell O'Connell he was wrong.' Again Illy was in a difficult position and unwisely he decided, rather than allowing Boycott to deliver half an apology, to go and do the job himself. It is sad that Geoff Boycott could not see that, whatever the justification, his ill-considered action had been indefensible; an unqualified and spontaneous apology would have prompted most fair-minded people to view his error, performed as it was in the heat of the moment, with a much greater degree of tolerance.

Illy was criticised for not enforcing the follow-on in this Adelaide Test, and it was even suggested that there was a suspicion of pique at the over-loading of the Test programme because of the agreement to play a seventh Test in place of the Melbourne match lost to the weather. He is adamant that the decision was made entirely for sound cricketing reasons, and *Wisden* supports this view. John Snow, the spearhead of the England attack, had bowled twenty-one eight-ball overs in the first innings and was near to exhaustion, while Peter Lever was not fully fit; when Bob Willis's extreme youth is also recalled it is not hard to see why Ray thought as he did. There was always the chance that Ian Chappell and Ken Stackpole might have savaged a tired and ragged attack so that jaded English batsmen would have been faced with Gleeson and Mallett and a considerable total in the fourth innings on a wicket sympathetic to spin. The ease with which Australia held out in their last knock proved these fears to have been groundless, but they were real enough at the time.

Victory by 62 runs in the seventh Test with its controversial 'walkabout' decided the Ashes and the Rubber; it also represented a personal triumph for Illy. He had bowled, batted and captained his side with single-minded skill and dedication. He had been sent by his country, as a professional cricketer, to achieve the hardest task that the game offers: he had won a series in Australia in the face of what he regarded as unsatisfactory umpiring and had been consistently harassed by criticism from a section of the press. Emotionally and physically drained he did not, even as a born fighter, possess the necessary energy and initiative to instigate legal procedings over one newspaper's handling of his letter of complaint over Lou Rowan. Having missed the story initially that the letter had been sent to the Australian Board, the cricket correspondent of a well-known evening paper apparently felt that stringent methods were called for. Illy was accused of leaking the news of the letter to the press. In fact it was another of the MCC party that told a London pressman; possibly prompted by a firm nudge from London, the correspondent first rang Richie Benaud who assured him that he had no chance of getting the contents of the letter. He then rang Illy who said, 'You know I can't tell you things like that. You obviously know that I'm complaining about Law 46', which was the law governing the use of persistent intimidation, the basic cause initially of the ill feeling between Illingworth and Rowan.

The next night a fictitious letter appeared in the newspaper under the signature, 'Yours sincerely, Ray Illingworth'. To say that this portrayed Ray in an unfavourable light is an understatement, and several senior MCC officials must have presumed him to be at fault until they visited Australia over a year later and saw the copy of the genuine letter that had been sent. At the press conference that followed the appearance of the fictitious letter, Illy was questioned on a curiously revealing phrase in it, 'the unfair tactics of the umpires', and he replied, 'That was not my letter.' The journalist called out, 'Oh, but I rang you about it, Ray.' Illy replied, 'That's not my letter and you know it,' but the journalist still seemed to suggest that it was the real letter that had been printed.

If one remembers the protracted legal squabblings and the eventual award of considerable damages to Knott and Illingworth over Denis Compton's allegations of cheating, it is clear that the pressman in question was a lucky man. As Ray put it, 'It was the end of the tour and I'd had a bellyful by then. I'm afraid I couldn't care less. He got his timing right but if he'd done it earlier in the tour it would have been an expensive error. I don't think the incident did me any good at Lord's.'

A win and a draw in the two Tests against New Zealand were tranquil affairs after the turbulence and Illy and his side returned home to find that their successes had not resulted in universal and unqualified delight. During the MCC v the Champion County match at Lord's, Billy Griffith came to the dressing room and asked Ray if he could have a few words with him after the days play at his house, which was close to the ground; Illy of course agreed and after having a couple of pints with the players arrived at Billy Griffith's house to find a reception committee consisting of Doug Insole, Sir Cyril Hawker and Griffith with papers in front of them and prepared to conduct what seemed to him to amount to an inquisition on the problems of the recent tour. Mentally unprepared, Illy felt that he gave as good as he got. One accusation rankled above all others. It was suggested that he had not handled John Snow as well as he should have done, to which Ray replied to the secretary of the MCC, 'You say that as a Sussex man! I've got more out of John Snow in four months than Sussex has got out of him in ten years.'

Illy's recollections of this meeting were very different from those of Billy Griffith, who thought it a good-humoured affair from which Ray emerged with considerable credit, different in every way from any sort of indictment.

At the celebration dinner at Lord's, held to mark the recapture of the Ashes, there appeared to be little real rejoicing. This occasioned Micky Stewart's remark to Illy that 'it seemed more like a funeral.' Veiled condemnation was forthcoming from the Cricket Council, which met on the last day of the MCC v Kent match and referred to 'grave concern about incidents involving dissent from umpires' decision whether by word or deed'. The statement went on, 'Whilst appreciating the strains and stresses under which cricket at the highest level is played, the Council must warn all players that such conduct, which is contrary to the spirit and tradition of the game and brings it into disrepute, will not be tolerated.'

Those who believe that the only alternative to standing up to the Australians and showing them, as Illy did, that you are as determined if not ruthless as they are, is to smile sweetly and lose found considerable consolation in the success of the 1970-1 MCC tour. Perhaps they had grown tired of seeing our sportsmen beaten if not humiliated in a variety of sports from skiing to golf and football. A little success came as a pleasant change.

16 The End Of The 'Illingworth Era'

The sound of dust settling can be both loud and prolonged. Press reaction to the 1970-1 Australian tour was sufficiently passionate and varied to suggest that general opinion in the country was equally divided. The populars, scenting the possibility of a ritual hanging, screamed support for Illy. He was, they affirmed, a hard professional cricketer captaining a team of hard professional cricketers and had been sent out to Australia to do a job. He had done it and now deserved nothing but praise, not condemnation.

The opposing view was that the Ashes had been regained but at considerable cost. Some of the tourists had not been dedicated ambassadors, had sometimes been churlish and quarrelsome, and consequently the image of English chricket had been adversely affected by the degree of controversy that the tour had engendered.

But Illy was back as England's captain for the home series against Pakistan and India in 1971, which helped to make cricketing history; on 24 August India registered their first victory in a Test match on English soil and with it the three-match series.

The first Test at Lord's will be principally remembered for 'The Gavaskar Incident'. *Wisden's* version of events is characteristically restrained: 'Soon after the start of the Indian second innings, when the game was crucially balanced, Gavaskar, racing to complete a quick single, was barged to the ground by Snow as the pair ran up the pitch together. It was an incident for which the England fast bowler was requested to apologise by both the chairman of selectors, Mr. A. V. Bedser, and Mr S. C. Griffith, secretary of the Test and County Cricket Board.' Illy certainly did not condone Snow's action but is quick to stress a different dimension of the ugly incident that was shown so regularly on television screens and discussed in acres of print. Within seconds there was laughter on the field, not at Gavaskar's expense but at the music-hall element that would have been appropriate in a knockabout clowning act but contrasted ludicrously with the dignity of a Lord's Test match.

In fact that night Sonny Gavaskar had a drink with John Snow and some of the England players, but Snow was dropped from England's team for the second Test at Manchester and the laughter did not erase the essential ugliness of the event. There was wild talk at the time of Billy Griffith being asked to leave the England dressing-room, and the subject has been dealt with in print in highly emotive terms by John Snow. Griffith himself is adamant that he has been misrepresented. His version of events generally tallies accurately with Illy's. As soon as Billy Griffith saw the barging of Gavaskar by Snow he went straight to Sir Cyril Hawker, who was President of the MCC, and asked him to demand an apology to the Indian side from Snow. Hawker's reply was, 'You'll do it so much better, Billy.' Having knocked on the dressing-room door, Griffith entered and asked if he could speak to the captain. Illy came out and they talked at the head of the stairs outside the dressing-room. At this stage, half way through the luncheon interval, Griffith did not know if Snow had apologised. He said to Illy, 'I must tell you that that was the most disgraceful thing that I've ever seen on a cricket field and for the sake of English cricket, he's got to go and apologise. Has he done so?'

Hearing that Snow had not apologised, Griffith asked Illingworth to tell Snow to go at once and do so; this Illy admits he was not prepared to do immediately. Griffith asked and received permission to re-enter the dressing-room, where he ordered Snow to apologise. Snow initially blustered refusal and Griffith had to say, 'It's not a question of what you want to do. You will do this and you will do it at once.' This was the only time during his many years as Secretary of the MCC that Billy Griffith ever had to issue a direct order to an England cricketer during a Test match. Snow's eventual apology was accepted by the tourists and the matter was closed.

Here again the contrast in the tactical and the strategic view-point is apparent. Illy appears to have been motivated by a cautious desire to avoid trouble with a key member of his side, while Griffith, acutely aware of the damage to English cricket and indeed cricket generally that the escalating publicity given to the barging incident could produce, was taking a much broader and more statesmanlike attitude. Perhaps, deep down, Illy may have registered the criticisms of over-reaction to trouble in taking his side off the field in the stormy seventh Test at Sydney and mistakenly moved towards the other extreme. Billy Griffith now is quite prepared to admit that he himself may have over-reacted to the situation but is uncompromising on the subject of his motives: 'At that time I had no other thought in my mind except the good of English cricket. Each time I saw the incident on television it looked worse. Somebody had to do something about it. I came into the dressing-room with the captain's permission, did what I had to do and left. To say that I was turned out of the dressing-room is a straight forward lie.'

Naturally there was a feeling of friction if not downright resentment between Illy and Griffith following this drama but, unlike Snow, who seems to have allowed resentment to fester over the years, Illy has apparently forgiven and forgotten. In Billy Griffith's own words, 'After the problems of the 70-1 Australian tour and the Gavaskar incident, I've always felt that Raymond and I have got on well. I appreciated the fact that he seemed to forget all about the troubles and refused to bear malice.'

Either side could have emerged from the Lord's Test as winners, but the match ended in a draw when rain intervened, though Farokh Engineer had hinted at the batting form that was to do so much to help India to victory at the Oval. There was pressure on Illy again at Old Trafford where England collapsed against Abid Ali's benevolent medium pace. He came in to bat with the score at 116 for 5 after Brian Luckhurst and Alan Knott had commenced the recovery with a stand of 75 for the fifth wicket; it was continued on the second day by Ray whose second Test century occupied four hours eighteen minutes, his partner-ship of 168 for the eighth wicket with Peter Lever being an

English record against India. Set to make 420 on a seamer's wicket, India must have appreciated the dreaded Manchester rain that prevented any play on the last day so that the sides met at the Oval on 19 August after two drawn games.

Illy must have smiled quietly at the irony of fate that brought Sir Leonard Hutton's son, Richard, the Yorkshire all-rounder, under his command at Manchester; Richard Hutton also played at the Oval, sharing in a marauding seventh wicket stand of 103 runs in sixty-six minutes with Alan Knott, which helped to leave India in some disarray, conceding a first-innings lead of 71; but that was the end of the good news as far as England were concerned. Ray had taken 5 for 70 in 34.3 overs in India's first innings, sure evidence that the pitch held encouragement to a spinner. Chandrasekhar with 6 for 38, well supported by Bedi and Venkataraghavan, bustled England out for 101 so that the tourists needed only 173 for victory. *Wisden* captures some of the excitement that held players and spectators alike: 'The tension was high and the Indians, avoiding all risks, took three hours to make the last 97 runs. Illingworth, in his own way, again bowled beautifully, but without luck; and his field placings were masterly, as was his handling of the attack.' Illy's figures in that dramatic second innings were 36 overs: 15 maidens: 40 runs: 0 wickets, and if Engineer, through characteristically cheerful improvisation, had not forcefully taken charge when his side had reached 134 for 5 England might just have wriggled out of their predicament.

A winter free of cricket in 1971-2 was particularly welcome to Illy owing to growing fatigue and business pressure. The demands of Test cricket, especially when allied to leadership at county level, and of family and business commitments could and did become immensely exacting; but energy and zest had returned when Ian Chappell's youthful and largely untried Australian tourists arrived the following summer.

The season commenced with arctic weather and regular rain but by the time of the first Test at Manchester victories against Worcestershire, Hampshire and MCC had prevented any hint of complacency in the English camp. Illy, again England's captain, must have thought long and hard on 8 June whether or not to

112

celebrate both his fortieth birthday and winning the toss by asking the Australians to bat first.

In the event, his decision to bat was followed by a patchy England performance apart from Tony Greig, in his first Test match, and John Edrich; England were all out for 249 but their seam attack without the aid of a single over from the spinners shot the tourists out for 142. England's grip never slackened with victory coming in mid-afternoon on the fifth day by 89 runs.

At Lord's the boomerang swing of Bob Massie claimed sixteen wickets in the match, the other four going to his hostile partner Dennis Lillee; England were swept to comprehensive defeat by eight wickets on the fourth day and it was clear that the emergence of both Lillee and Greg Chappell as indisputably world-class players in this crushing Australian victory would assume infinite significance in the future.

The third Test was played at Nottingham, and on winning the toss Illy sent the Australians in to bat; his decision was widely believed to have been motivated by a canny wish to keep his rather fragile batting away from the triumphant Australian pace attack of Lillee and Massie for as long as possible. Brian Bolus, the Nottinghamshire captain and Ray's former Yorkshire colleague, advised him that the wicket could be expected to become progressively slower and easier, but a sound first innings total of 315 by Australia was followed by England's eclipse, again at the hands of Lillee and Massie. They were all out for 189 and it needed a dedicated rearguard action in their second innings to earn a draw.

Thus it was in the context of appreciable if not decisive Australian psychological ascendancy that the sides met at Leeds. Australia, sensing the type of pitch to be expected, substituted Mallett for Gleeson, and Derek Underwood, who had been out of favour, was preferred to Norman Gifford. In this match the constitution of the turf was as unkind as the elements had been at Manchester, and spectators were regaled with the unusual spectacle of two spinners, Underwood and Illingworth, operating on the first morning of a Test match.

Snow made the breakthrough when he had Ross Edwards

caught behind in the first over, but before Underwood tore the heart out of the tourists' batting it was Illy who dismissed the Chappell brothers, Ian caught and bowled and Greg leg before, to decimate the early batting. He also helped Underwood to his excellent return of 4 for 37 off 31 overs by catching Marsh at mid-on off a skier and bringing off a brilliant one-handed catch at point to dismiss Sheahan.

The degree of help to spin bowling provided by this Headingley wicket guaranteed conjecture and suspicion. Had the wicket been fashioned for Underwood? Bill Bowes, writing in *Wisden*, is in no doubt: 'Not for a moment would one suggest that conditions had been deliberately engineered . . . but the fact remained, that they were conditions least likely to help the tourists.' England still had to demonstrate superior technique in dealing with the turning ball and had it not been for their two top scorers, Ray Illingworth (57) and John Snow (48), coming in at numbers eight and nine the England lead, to which 'Mr Extras' contributed significantly with 46, would have been negligible. Illy's knock occupied four and a half hours and if ever a fighting, grafting innings was played for his side, this was it. Wholly demoralised, Australia collapsed again in the second innings for 136, with Underwood taking 6 for 45, leaving England only 20 for victory and the retention of the Ashes.

Lillee, with ten wickets in the match, and the Chappell brothers, who both scored first-innings centuries, restored Australian morale at the Oval, victory by five wickets to square the rubber coming with half a day to spare.

Illy, feeling the strain at the end of what had been a very demanding season, informed the selectors that he would not be available for the tour of India and Pakistan in 1972-3. He was therefore able to accept in person the CBE he had gained in the New Year's Honours' List, awarded for services to cricket.

Tony Lewis did an excellent job in India, but the selectors turned to Ray again in the summer as England's captain for the two short series against New Zealand and West Indies, and it was sad that, after he had served his country so well, his reign should end on a note of disastrous anti-climax.

New Zealand's test record of two losses and a draw was highly flattering to England, failing to reveal the very real likelihood of victory for the tourists both at Trent Bridge and Lord's; in the first Test, Illy set New Zealand 479 for victory and there have been few more gallant performances in recent international cricket than their remarkable response in scoring 440, admittedly on a wicket that was less helpful to seam bowling than it had been earlier in the match. Illy failed to take a single wicket in the three Tests and, having averaged only twenty with the bat, could hardly regard the series as a personal triumph.

Worse was to follow. West Indian cricket had been ailing at international level for about seven years, but England managed to revive the patient. Despite a better personal performance from Ray, England lost the first Test at the Oval by 158 runs, and after drawing at Edgbaston the sides met at Lords where West Indies won the toss and plundered 652 for 8 declared before Holder, Boyce and Gibbs with some aid from Julien in the second innings bowled England out twice to win by the shattering margin of an innings and 226 runs. Illy's comment at the close of an embarrassingly one-sided contest was as blunt as it was truthful. 'We were outbatted, outbowled and outfielded. There are no excuses.'

The match will also be remembered as Raymond Illingworth's last as England's captain. The selectors were to announce the MCC captaincy for the following winter's tour of the West Indies, and general opinion in the media as well as the corridors of power suggested that Illy would be retained. During the Saturday, however, Alec Bedser came to Illy and told him that he had not got the job. Bedser seemed perturbed and the words he used were, 'I'm very sorry indeed and some day I'll tell you all about it.' He is still waiting to hear 'all about it'.

No one could argue that his sacking was caused by the magnitude of the West Indies' win at Lord's, for when the news was given to Illy England were only part way through their first innings. A stronger argument was that he was regarded as insufficiently diplomatic to guarantee a smooth and trouble-free tour in volatile and potentially explosive circumstances. What *Wisden* called the 'Illingworth era' was over.

He had led England in thirty-six Tests, had won back and

retained the Ashes and, whatever his critics might say, had commanded the respect and loyalty of the players under him; in addition his own playing talent as a Test cricketer could no longer be questioned, and as a tactician he had proved himself to have few, if any, equals. Utterly unsentimental and realistic he had predictably projected a down-to-earth, utilitarian image. In 1975, when Leicestershire were in clear sight of their first championship, they were set a taxing declaration by Lancashire's captain, David Lloyd, at Blackpool. Ray was standing outside the dressing room with his pads on, and an old gentleman who was a passionate Leicestershire supporter called up to him, 'Win for us, Ray!' Illy replied cheerfully, 'We'll try to win for us bloody selves!' The answer tells one a great deal about the man.

17 Leicestershire's Gain

It might come as something of a surprise to those who have known him down the years to discover that Illy sees himself as a generally broad-minded and liberal man. When asked recently about some problem or confrontation during his controversial reign as England's captain, he replied, 'I always wanted to get some agreement out of any situation. I suppose I could be bloody-minded,' and, being a realist, he added, 'if the other feller was bloody-minded too then we might be a bit stuck!'

On his arrival at Leicestershire in 1969 it came as a genuine surprise that no one appeared to want to be 'bloody-minded' or, indeed, anything but co-operative and helpful, so that improvement based on 100 per cent effort from a dedicated team on and off the field meant that the old days when Leicestershire were something of a pushover fast receded into obscurity.

A key figure in their renaissance was Mike Turner, formerly a Leicestershire player, who for the last eighteen years has been their secretary. One must admire Yorkshire's courage in its own conviction that only native-born players may represent the county, but if a side is to be built over the years through shrewd signings of players from overseas as well as from other counties then it is as well to have a man of Turner's intelligence and experience in charge. His first major *coup* was unquestionably the signing of Tony Lock, mercurial, explosive and undeniably inspiring. Under him Leicestershire suddenly realised that there was no law against winning, a fact that appeared previously to have escaped them. In Lock's last season, 1967, they finished level with Kent as Championship runners-up to Yorkshire; this was easily the best showing the county had managed since Charlie Palmer's side had finished third in 1953.

Lock's volatile, excitable style of leadership was not to everyone's taste. The story went the rounds during his reign of a senior Leicestershire pro who dropped a catch; when a colleague inquired why the error had occurred he replied, 'I wasn't going to have that bloody Lockie kissing me!' But Tony Lock's reformed, jerkless, smooth-line action proved remarkably effective in 1967 and only Tom Cartwright and Derek Underwood took more first-class wickets that summer, after which he finished comfortably head of the Leicestershire bowling averages with 122 wickets at 18.11 apiece.

Virtually without warning, however, Lock decided to retire from English first-class cricket and the lack of his dynamic leadership and hostile bowling was reflected in a fall from second equal in 1967 to ninth in the Championship in 1968. But after the arrival of Ray Illingworth and Graham McKenzie at Grace Road in 1969 hopes were high.

Illy recalls vividly how he responded to an atmosphere and a régime that was infinitely more relaxed than the one that he had left after seventeen years. Happily he and Mike Turner struck up a pleasant, mutually respectful relationship from the outset, and it was during one of Ray's first visits to Grace Road in the winter prior to his first season that Turner asked him if he would like to captain the side, having sensed that Illy had exerted the keen intelligence of an *éminence grise* during Brian Close's time as Yorkshire captain. This represented a new challenge to Illy, who was glad to accept on condition that he would both make and take responsibility for the day-to-day decisions that only a captain can be expected to understand fully; he also made it clear from the outset that if the committee did not approve of his record and approach at the end of the season he would be perfectly happy to play under someone else's captaincy in the following year.

Selection procedure was crucial. In Yorkshire a large and therefore unwieldy committee had picked the sides, whereas at Leicester only a chairman, another committee member, Mike Turner, Raymond and the senior professional did the job. They would meet at the commencement of the season to discuss policy and thereafter, barring specific problems or a run of particularly bad form, selection would be left to Illy, working in close harness with Mike Turner in his capacity as team-manager. This approach is logical. Only a captain of a side can know what instructions have been given to a batsman and whether he has obeyed those instructions; anyone who does not see the side in action every match is bound to be tempted to judge a player on averages. In Ray's own words, 'It's only me that knows whether I've asked a batsman to get on with it and he's got out trying to do what he's told. Now he should know he's not going to be dropped. But if a player refuses to do what he's asked and plays for himself and not his side then he should know he may be dropped.'

One occasion when Illy asked for a meeting of the selection committee during a season was in the Championship year, 1975, when a spell of indifferent form necessitated the dropping of Graham McKenzie. Mike Turner and the committee backed him 100 per cent, as they did over the question of nets. The first two deliveries that Ray received in the Grace Road nets in 1969 exploded more or less off a length and shot straight over his head. Illy's reaction was to suspend the practice and to go directly in to Mike Turner with the firm request that as soon as ever possible the standard of the net wickets should be brought up to that of the square; it was not long before things were put right.

Another pleasing factor was the relationship between players and committee. Congratulation or commiseration in success or failure seemed to be wholly sincere and there was no suspicion of a gulf between dressing-room and committee room.

It was among the playing staff that Illy found a need to foster confidence and improved morale. Most of the players did not seem to believe in themselves or their own ability; after the considerable success of 1967, things had slipped back to the stage at which a Leicestershire cricketer's attitude might be summed up in the words, 'Let's go out there and enjoy ourselves. I know we aren't going to win anything but at least we're one of the best social sides in the country.' They knew at once that the new captain was really in charge. Fitness, the absolute need for dedicated, concentrated effort, punctuality and self-discipline were all stressed, and concern with higher standards of fielding and running between wickets achieved an improvement in morale and performance.

Leadership suited Illy, and as Leicestershire, exploiting a superb start to the season, found themselves once again close to the Championship table's head it was apparent that a new spirit was operating in the club; but as so often advance was followed by withdrawal. By early June Leicestershire were unbeaten with a couple of victories to their credit when Colin Cowdrey's injury prompted the selectors to call on Ray to lead England. He was away for six Test matches, Barry Knight for five, and when he returned for periodic matches Illy sensed strongly that the positive, confident team spirit that he had worked to encourage had virtually evaporated. Leicestershire won only two more Championship matches in the remainder of the season (Illy was playing in both of them) and sunk sadly to a position of four-teenth in the final table. Ray, not given to making extravagent claims, still felt that if he had played every match for his new county they would have headed or come close to heading the Championship table in his first season.

His colleagues had glimpsed the attacking potential of his bowling in the first Championship match of the season. Both the first and the last day of Warwickshire's visit to Grace Road were lost to the rain, but on Monday, 12 May Illy casually swept aside a powerful batting side almost single-handed with a return of 7 for 27 off 21 skilfully-spun and flighted overs; five weeks later he celebrated victory over West Indies in his first Test as England's captain by returning to his new county side and plundering 153 not out against Essex, a county that he had consistently put to the sword during his days with Yorkshire. Doubtless Messrs Lever, Turner, East, Ackfield and Hobbs were heartily sick of the sight of him.

Ray finished top of both batting and bowling averages for Leicestershire at the close of his first season, but this could not hide the fact that overall it had been a thoroughly disappointing year both in the Championship and in the one-day game. It was this 1969 season that saw the inauguration of the John Player County League, and Leicestershire, apparently well-equipped for one-day cricket, finished eleventh in addition to losing to Sussex in the quarter-finals of the Gillette Cup (a competition that generally had not brought the best out of them).

But Ray's Farsley days in the Bradford League were not so far off that he found difficulty in applying the principles upon which success in limited-overs cricket is based. They came seventh in the Sunday League in 1970, fourth in 1971 and second in 1972, an upward progression based on shrewd captaincy, improved fielding and running between wickets and increasingly tight bowling to a preconceived plan; even in the early days at Leicester, Raymond used spinners far more in the one-day game than most county captains, knowing well, and often demonstrating the fact himself, that an accurate spinner, bowling to his field, is generally harder to score off than all but the best medium-pace bowler pegging away at the middle stump.

Peter Marner and Clive Inman, both fine players who appeared to have lost something of their appetite for the game, retired in the early 1970s, making way for Brian Davison and Chris Balderstone, who have been at the heart of Leicestershire's successes. But the steady progress in limited-overs cricket was not reflected in any marked improvement in the Championship. The truth was of course that Illy, still missing about half the county's three-day matches owing to Test cricket, had managed to establish a tactical grasp that would operate efficiently enough in his absence in a forty-over match; when he missed a Championship game, Leicestershire were a different side.

These were challenging and enjoyable days in which new vistas unfolded in terms of leadership at county and international level. It would have been surprising if success at Leicester had come instantly; nevertheless the seeds of later triumphs were sown in these early days and not least in the development of Illy's relationship with Mike Turner into genuine friendship.

Visits to Leicester by Ray's wife, Shirley, and their two girls, Vicki and Diane, were eagerly anticipated and enjoyed; probably he saw as much of them as he did during his Yorkshire days, as all Leicestershire's home games are played at Grace Road, whereas many of Yorkshire's 'home' games necessitated a considerable amount of travel. Naturally enough the question of whether the family should pack its bags and move down to the Midlands arose. Illy would at this stage have been very happy to do so, but the collective decision to remain in Yorkshire was taken and the Illingworths stayed during home matches at the Grand Hotel in Leicester until escalating prices caused a recent change to a rented house.

As Illy's reputation as an international cricketer and captain grew, so the players predictably formed a loyal and integrated group behind him, reacting to his straight, blunt talking and transparent concern with their interests. Out of his intelligent leadership off and on the field, allied to Mike Turner's shrewd administration and consistent support, was fashioned the balanced, competitive, disciplined unit that was to prove itself to be one of the most consistently successful county sides of the 1970s.

18 Slopes And Summit

In 1972 Leicestershire won the Benson and Hedges Cup in its inaugural year. It would be hard to exaggerate the significance of this success in the new world of big-money, one-day cricket; apart from providing further evidence for confidence in the county's leadership, the waverers who demand a Cup or League triumph in exchange for their allegiance began to be assuaged, and gates at Grace Road improved accordingly.

The Australian selectors who omitted Graham McKenzie from the touring party for that season so that he was available for his adopted county were ironically among Leicestershire's most sympathetic and co-operative helpers. Illy, using him as spearhead, found an able partner in Ken Higgs who arrived at Grace Road after a short period in the Lancashire League; these two were responsible for crucial contributions in both the Benson and Hedges Cup and the John Player Sunday League, in which Leicestershire, beaten by Yorkshire in their final match by three runs, finished as runners-up, only a single point behind Kent.

Terry Spencer also bowled with much of his old hostility, and with the usual hand of spinners Leicestershire were probably better equipped in attack for the limited-overs game than any other county. They headed the Midland Zone, unbeaten in the qualifying matches, and had fashioned a distinctive pattern of batting in which their canny opener, Mick Norman, would pace the innings as anchor-man while the explosive Brian Davison or Roger Tolchard, fed with the strike and confident of Leicestershire's depth in batting, could frolic freely. Any combination of these three represented a classic lesson in the art of running and calling; runs were harvested where none seemed to exist, and, allied to excellent fielding, matches were consequently won that could so easily have been lost.

In the quarter-finals Lancashire were drawn to meet Leicestershire at Grace Road, and a batting line-up that contained Clive and David Lloyd, Barry Wood and Farokh Engineer, with a player of Jack Simmons ability coming in at number nine, was not to be underestimated. As in the Leeds Test in 1969, Ray took the crucial wicket of Clive Lloyd and, in dismissing Ken Snellgrove and Barry Wood to take 3 for 30 off 10 overs, must have been a serious candidate for the Gold Award. But some fine batting from Barry Duddleston who helped to guide Leicestershire to a seven-wicket victory earned him the adjudicator's decision.

Leicestershire again won by seven wickets in the semi-final, this time at Warwickshire's expense. Illy, who took 3 for 19 off 11 mean overs, was given the Gold Award by his old colleague Len Hutton, who appreciated the value of thrift as much as its recipient. Ray learnt that his opponents in the final at Lord's on 22 July were to be Yorkshire.

Whenever he opens a paper at his breakfast table during the cricket season, Illy glances at the match in which he is playing and immediately his eyes slide from Leicestershire's match to Yorkshire's. The habits of seventeen years of apprenticeship, development and maturity do not die easily; Illy would not have been human if he had faced a confrontation between his new county and his old with relaxed objectivity.

In the event Leicestershire won comfortably enough. Geoff Boycott was out of the Yorkshire side owing to a hand injury (he celebrated his return to first-class cricket in early August with a double century against Leicestershire in Illy's absence), and no Yorkshireman fully mastered Leicestershire's varied and well-handled attack in difficult conditions. Despite the weight of rain that fell early in the day, play began on time; Philip Sharpe won the toss and Yorkshire batted. Higgs, McKenzie and Spencer chipped away at the early batting with Barry Leadbeater suffering a painful crack on the wrist from Spencer that made him retire. He returned late in the innings and contributed Yorkshire's top score before being run out, but Illy removed John Woodford and the potentially punishing Chris Old in a crucial spell that earned him 2 for 21 off 10 overs.

Yorkshire had struggled. Would Leicestershire find the going any easier? Once again Mick Norman paced the innings precisely after the early loss of Barry Dudleston and the two most attacking batsmen in the side, Roger Tolchard and Brian Davison. One former Yorkshireman had helped to bowl his former county towards defeat. Another, Chris Balderstone, now batted with a confidence and freedom that left the issue in no doubt.

Having helped England to retain the Ashes, Illy led Leicestershire to their first major triumph, the Benson and Hedges trophy, and watched them falter by those three crucial runs that cost them the Sunday League; he finished the 1972 season a tired but an immensely proud and happy man.

The next season represented the trough that so often follows a crest. Defeated in the quarter-finals of the Benson and Hedges Cup, Leicestershire finished fifth in the Sunday League, ninth in the Championship and went out of the Gillette Cup in the third round; not a disastrous showing but hardly what the heady successes of the previous year had encouraged their supporters to anticipate. Illy, as disappointed as any, reflected that loss of the England captaincy to Mike Denness, following an indifferent performance against New Zealand and annihilation by West Indies, would mean that Leicestershire would have his undivided attention and energy at their disposal in 1974. The result was spectacular.

Beaten finalists in the Benson and Hedges Cup, Leicestershire won the John Player Sunday League for the first time and actually contributed five of the first sixteen in the League batting averages; even more significantly, they improved their County Championship position to fourth, aided by magnificent form from Brian Davison and the newly-arrived Norman McVicker, who had been specially registered from Warwickshire. If Balderstone, second in the county batting and top of their bowling averages, had not returned to his footballing duties with Carlisle during July, they might well have finished even higher.

The following year Leicestershire cruised to victory in their second successive Benson and Hedges Cup final, beating Middlesex by five wickets after dismissing them for 146 through the usual mixture of tight bowling, athletic fielding and Illy's shrewd captaincy. Ted Dexter's decision to name Norman

McVicker, Leicestershire's hugely successful tail-end batsman and seam bowler, was prophetic. No one, Illy apart, had a greater influence on the winning of their first championship in the ninety-six years' history of the club.

Leicestershire hardly started the 1975 season like champions. Three drawn matches were followed by a comfortable victory by 143 runs over Northants at Grace Road, but the fuse only began to smoulder in mid-June. Somerset, Hampshire and Glamorgan were all beaten and the only set-back to the county's cheerful progress occurred at the Oval at the beginning of July. Illy, who contributed the first hat-trick in his twenty-four years of first-class cricket, could not prevent defeat for his side after they had been dismissed for 68 in the first innings and followed on, scoring 283 to leave Surrey requiring 92 for victory. To their credit, Leicestershire, for whom Illy took 4 for 20, bowled Surrey to 65 for 9, but Intikhab and Pocock guided them to their narrow victory.

The rest of the season, apart from drawn games against Lancashire and Derbyshire, was all sunlit uplands and birdsong; Derbyshire, who were outplayed for the whole match, had only one wicket intact when rain intervened. The days as late as mid-June when only Gloucestershire stood below them in the table were soon forgotten.

A hint of what was to come occurred in their stirring victory against the Australians at Grace Road. The match was played immediately prior to the second Test and Brian Davison annihilated the tourists, admittedly in the absence of Lillee and Thomson, with a superb 189, easily his highest first-class score. Illy removed three of the tourist's front-line batsmen in the second innings and Leicestershire won by 31 runs after Ray's declaration had required them to score 275 in four hours and forty minutes.

Now his fine team appeared to be invincible. Problems and adversity still lay ahead but there always seemed to be the corporate spirit and the inspired individual to provide the answer. The first of the six consecutive victories that brought Leicestershire their Championship was against Nottinghamshire at Grace Road. The fierce onslaught of Davison and

Balderstone, who added 305 for the third wicket, was the prelude to victory by an innings and nine runs after Illy, Balderstone and Birkenshaw, bowling into the rough, had taken nine of the Notts second-innings wickets; at Northampton, Illy followed an unbeaten 73 on a lively wicket with second innings figures of 5 for 20, greatly aided by Norman McVicker's half century at number nine, so that good batting from John Steele and Chris Balderstone saw Leicestershire safely home by nine wickets.

Again it was Norman McVicker who came in as nightwatchman and hit a career best 73 in Leicestershire's first innings against Nottinghamshire at Trent Bridge, which helped to earn a substantial first-innings lead and eventual victory by eight wickets; Illy, again pitching in the stud marks obligingly scuffed by Nottinghamshire's left arm quickie, Barry Stead, had taken 4 for 48 in 25 overs in their second innings. (Barry Stead was born in Leeds and his assistance in this crucial win, however, unintentional, might have prompted the reaction that Yorkshire blood is thicker than water!)

Perhaps the greatest match of the final six was played against Kent at Tunbridge Wells. There was something in the Neville wicket for bowlers during the entire match and it was again the amazing McVicker, sharing in a ninth-wicket stand of 136 with Graham McKenzie, who swung the game Leicestershire's way. Illy, who captained with all his customary shrewdness and enterprise, was again among the wickets, taking 4 for 42 off 17 overs, but without McKenzie and McVicker, who contributed over half Leicestershire's runs, this match would surely have been lost, as Kent, needing only 202 to win, reached 160 for 4 before Illy's incisive spin really began to bite.

Middlesex, in time-honoured constabulary phrase, came quietly in the penultimate match, and Leicestershire, with five successive wins to their credit, travelled to Chesterfield, needing seven points from Derbyshire to earn the most coveted award in county cricket.

Leicestershire first led the table on 5 September and with ultimate success so tantalisingly close it was a taxing decision for Illy when he won the toss and saw a considerable degree of green in the Queen's Park wicket; should he put Derbyshire in and hope to exploit what events might prove to be the most favourable bowling conditions of the match? On the other hand, the cutting edge of his attack was seriously blunted. Ken Higgs had been bowling with his foot strapped for four matches which restricted his crucial delivery stride. (In Illy's words, 'Ken loses a lot of pace and bounce if he can't bang his foot down when he bowls.') The other problem was that Graham McKenzie, who had been dropped during the latter part of the season for indifferent form, was something of an unknown factor; might Leicestershire be asking the lion-hearted McVicker to shoulder more responsibility than even he could carry?

Illy decided to bat. He then went across to the press box and called to Martin Johnson of the *Leicester Mercury*: 'I've just had an interesting conversation with the groundsman. Why don't you go and have a word with him?' Martin went out to the square where the gentleman in question replied to his comment on the greenness of the wicket: 'Green? Of course it's green. I'm the park-keeper and it's more than my job's worth to leave nasty brown patches around. The folks come to picnic and feed the ducks and they like to see lots of green all around them!'

The first innings opened shakily and then deteriorated! Three wickets fell to the Derbyshire pace attack of Alan Ward, Mike Hendrick and Philip Russell. Soon Leicestershire became 49 for 5, but Illy fought them off long enough after the luncheon interval for the wicket to ease appreciably. By mid-afternoon the ball was seaming less and the bounce was more predictable. Leicestershire's lowest point was 77 for 6. McKenzie finished with 44 not out, and helped by useful contributions from Jeff Tolchard and Jack Birkenshaw, followed by a last wicket stand of 37, Leicestershire were all out for an admittedly disappointing first innings total of 226, which could so easily have failed to reach three figures.

In reply, Derbyshire reached 41 without loss by the close, and next morning Illy, examining the wicket for signs of renewed freshness provided by the September dew, was horrified to find it dry, brown and therefore probably placid; if Derbyshire had been a really good batting side, Leicestershire might have been in real trouble. After Norman McVicker had nipped out the openers, Illy took 4 for 31 to decimate the middle order, and when Derbyshire were all out the prospective champions had earned a slender lead; but the four bowling points they had achieved in the process had brought them the Championship by default as their nearest rivals were frustrated either by the weather or by their opponents.

There was more drama in Chris Balderstone's hurried departure, plus attendant mobile television cameras, on a swift dash northwards to play football for Doncaster Rovers that evening; he had been on the field for the entire six and a half hours' play, less eight minutes, and had 51 not out to his name when the last over was bowled. Before his hurried journey the fall of a Leicestershire wicket had occasioned the enquiry among the press: 'Was he caught in midfield?'

That night the Leicestershire players dined together at their Chesterfield hotel and enjoyed the wine sent in honour of their achievement by some well-wishers, but it was no all night carousel. Most were too tired and were in bed before midnight. The following morning there was a hard frost and the wicket was again lively and taxing. With the Championship safely won, Illy's professionalism and that of his side demanded continued effort and dedication. Chris Balderstone, who had the previous day achieved the rare if not unique distinction of being the only person ever to play first-class cricket and League football on the same day, completed a fine century and, ending the season in the grand manner, Leicestershire bowled Derbyshire out with just five minutes to spare, to win by 135 runs.

As ever on these occasions speeches and champagne flowed freely, and one ecstatic Leicestershire supporter, moved by joy and by an excess of celebratory beverages, was observed to collapse on a length in the middle of the wicket that had just been used, babbling happily.

During his long and distinguished career with Yorkshire, the County Championship had been claimed, as by right, no less than seven times. Five times Yorkshire had finished as runners-up, usually to Surrey. Predictably Illy admitted that the winning of this Championship had given him more pleasure than any of the others. Many would agree that it was his finest accomplishment.

19 Conclusion

What a time September 1975 would have been for Illy to announce his retirement, the plaudits of press and public ringing in his ears; but such a move would have smacked of the theatrical and there are few less dramatic individuals in England.

Instead he continued and, as I write in 1977, continues his career as a professional cricketer; his benefit seems certain to break all records for his county, and Leicestershire's successes, though not quite emulating the peaks of 1975, have continued. In the 1976 season the county finished fourth in the Championship and at the head of the John Player League with points equal to four other counties. Leicestershire, suffering from the rule that was to benefit them the following season, had to content themselves with a share of third place. They had only four wins to Essex's and Kent's five, and poor Essex, still tying with Kent on the number of away wins, conceded the league title by virtue of Kent's faster overall scoring-rate by 0.42 of a run!

Essex County Cricket Club began its career in 1876 and victory in its centenary would have been doubly welcome. A year later it is still without a major trophy or championship; Leicestershire were the beneficiaries in 1977, finishing equal on points and taking the Sunday League title because they had registered one victory more than Essex. Ironically it was Yorkshire, defeating Essex at Scarborough in the penultimate match, that set up the situation from which Illy and his men could register a triumph that had earlier seemed to have slipped away from them.

Leicestershire's cause was not furthered by the inordinate number of injuries that they suffered, including an incredible ten fractures to various members of the first-team squad. They finished fifth in the 1977 Championship nevertheless, and a disappointing performance in the Benson and Hedges Cup was partly offset by improved showing in the Gillette Cup, though

131

they lost a rain-affected semi-final to Glamorgan; the real possibility of Brian Close and Raymond Illingworth leading out their adopted counties in the final at Lord's had been captivating the cricketing world; Glamorgan's victory defied both common sense and the form book, though Middlesex's win over Somerset was more readily predictable.

Illy's own form may not have been spectacular, but there were occasions when the old magic was as apparent as ever; none was more remarkable than his last-wicket stand with his vice-captain, Ken Higgs, against Northamptonshire at Grace Road on Monday, 29 August. Higgs himself a sprightly stripling in his forty-first year, joined his captain with Leicestershire's score at a grotesque 45 for 9 on a wicket that had given the Northants seamers considerable help.

When they were parted, 228 runs had been added, easily the largest last-wicket stand ever made for the county and only seven runs short of the highest ever in the County Championship, between Woolley and Fielder for Kent against Worcestershire in 1909. Higgs, who had never scored a first-class century, became noticeably restless in the nineties and, attempting an ambitious single into the covers, was run out two short of his hundred. What Illy said to him as they limped back to the pavilion is not on record. Perhaps he adapted another famous Yorkshireman's comment in roughly similar circumstances: 'Thee and tha fancy singles at tha time of life!' Illy was 119 not out and Leicestershire, all out for 273, had turned apparent disaster into a first innings lead of 101.

But the 1977 season will be remembered primarily by enthusiast, player and historian alike as the year when Kerry Packer, predatory as an eagle but lacking the bird's inherent nobility, stooped on cricket with a suddenness and ferocity that left the sporting world utterly bemused.

Will cricket, which had already been moving steadily towards the ethos of professional football before the cataclysm, ever be quite the same again? Will gimmick, crowd-pleasing, artificiality as marked in the play itself as in the prefabricated conditions and, above all, the lack of genuine patriotic involvement that the alleged 'World Series' invites, guarantee its eventual or indeed immediate failure, leaving Packer and cricket itself joint losers?

The story is often told of the American visitor to Cambridge who greatly admired the wonderful sweep of turf that is such a feature of King's as you enter the College from King's Parade. Chancing to meet the head gardener, he enquired how such turf could be cultivated. 'It's quite simple,' was the reply. 'You keep on cutting, rolling, watering and tending the grass for four or five hundred years!' How can a wicket worthy of the world's best players, or indeed able to reassure them with regard to reasonable standards of safety, be created over a period of a few months in large trays, suitable for the production of mushrooms or forced lettuces?

Predictably Illy is ambivalent in his attitude to the whole sorry muddle. 'If someone had come along to me and offered me twenty or thirty thousand pounds for a couple of years cricket at the end of my career, I'd have had to think very hard. I didn't get an offer so I've never had to face the problem; but I don't believe that what Packer is going to serve up will be cricket as we know it and I'm worried about the general effect on the game.'

Always a man to weigh his words with meticulous care, he might well be guilty in this case of considerable understatement. How long will it be before the star player *has* to score runs, and the fielders will therefore conveniently 'drop' him, as one has so often seen in festival, exhibition or benefit matches? Just how fiercely will the tail-ender be assailed with bouncers? When will huge cardboard hands clap on a grotesque scoreboard or 'appropriate' music accompany the performance of the players as in baseball? To those of us who believe that the most apt music with which to garnish Mr Packer's fare is a funeral march, his whole, admittedly open, attempt to commercialise cricket totally and irrevocably can only represent a potentially disastrous threat.

Sadly this may not be apparent to many club and village cricketers or even to the present generation of Farsley Juniors; between Long Room and little wooden pavilion there is a great gulf fixed, and it may well be that the reaction of the establishment as it gathered its skirts in horror at Packer's advances appears irrelevant to the future of cricket at grassroots level.

My basic premise has been throughout that Illy represents the meeting-ground in the game of the old and the new; he knew well the bad, old days of near-penury and insecurity and, though he welcomes it, he knows equally well the dangers attendant on vast sums of money sunk in sport. Cricketers at any level would do well to heed his muted warning on the subject of Kerry Packer.

His critics will not want to listen. They will judge him in their own way, perhaps on the sort of incident in the earlier part of his career that occurred on the 1962-3 MCC tour of Australia under the captaincy of Ted Dexter and the managership of the Duke of Norfolk; state duties at home required the Duke's departure from Australia in mid-tour and a brief illness meant that he was in England for as much as six weeks, during which time his place as tour-manager was taken by Billy Griffith.

A combination of injury on the field and indisposition off it during the third Test at Sydney, for which Illy had not been selected, suddenly presented Griffith with the realisation that England did not at one stage possess a twelfth man! The only member of the party unaccounted for who could perform the duties of twelfth man was Raymond Illingworth, and he was not even at the ground. Alarums and excursions were followed by his being run to earth at the hotel where the team were staying, apparently oblivious of the fact that loyalty to his captain and colleagues demanded his presence at a crucial Test Match.

Another side to Illy's character, however, can be illustrated by his old friend and mentor Eddie Hargrave. We commenced our search for an understanding of Raymond Illingworth, the man and the cricketer, in Farsley. Let us end it there. Hargrave recalls that Illy invited him to both civic receptions on the occasion of his first Test Match and the winning of the Ashes under his captaincy. 'He remembered me when he was up there and I was down here and I'm grateful.'

Harry Bailes, the first captain whom Illy played under for Farsley in the Bradford League, always carries with him a cutting in which Illy acknowledges the debt that he owed Harry from his earliest cricketing days. 'Ah were t'captain that put him on t'bowl first.' Harry Bailes's rich accent makes the word

134

'bowl' rhyme with 'howl'. 'He's never got swelled-headed and his feet have never left t'ground. He remembered us after 'e'd got famous. Ah don't think as 'e's ever growed away from this village.'

Eddie Hargrave recalled a Sunday match years ago. 'It were Bradford Junior League against Airedale Junior League. Brian Close played and honestly they didn't mek a cap big enough in Leeds to fit 'im but 'e were a hundred per cent trier like Raymond and it were a good thing for both of them that they left Yorkshire.'

Without emigrating south to Leicestershire, Illy might never have enjoyed the opportunity to develop his gifts of leadership; it is inconceivable to picture him in any role other than that of a professional cricketer, but it does not require much imagination to visualise him as a frustrated man at the end of his career who knew that he had failed to realise his full potential. Success, chiefly in the form of the Leicestershire and England captaincies, has dealt kindly with Illy, and much of the early abrasiveness has departed through an impressive mellowing which has done nothing to blunt his keen competitive edge; thus the tactician has become the strategist; the poacher is now the gamekeeper and the shop-steward has developed towards the statesman.

When voices are raised in the future over the shape, policies and development of cricket, it is to be hoped that Illy's will be among them and that he will be heeded.

He knows and understands the pressures and dangers of the arena but he has not forgotten, nor will he ever forget, the sight-screen at Farsley Cricket Club.